VERMONT

Newport

St. Albans

89
7

2

Lake
Champlain

Mt. Mansfield
(4,393 ft) ▲

Essex
Junction

Winooski
Burlington
South Burlington

Barton R.

Lake
Willoughby

5

St. Johnsbury

Connecticut R.

Connecticut R.

2

Winooski R.

Montpelier ◉

Barre

91

7

Vergennes

Otter R.

Middlebury

Green Mtn.
National
Forest

89

Lake
Bomoseen

4

Rutland

4

White River
Junction

Poultney R.

Otter R.

91

Connecticut R.

Metlauee R.

Green Mtn.
National
Forest

Bellows Falls

7

Bennington

Brattleboro

**VERMONT
BY ROAD**

CELEBRATE THE STATES
VERMONT

Dan Elish

BENCHMARK BOOKS

MARSHALL CAVENDISH
NEW YORK

Benchmark Books
Marshall Cavendish Corporation
99 White Plains Road
Tarrytown, New York 10591-9001

Copyright © 1997 by Marshall Cavendish Corporation

Library of Congress Cataloging-in-Publication Data
Elish, Dan.
Vermont / Dan Elish.
p.   cm. — (Celebrate the states ; 2)
Includes bibliographical references and index.
Summary: Surveys the geography, history, government, customs, and people of the state of Vermont
ISBN 0-7614-0146-6 (lib. bdg.)
1. Vermont—Juvenile literature. [1. Vermont.] I. Title. II. Series.
F49.3.E45   1997   974.3—dc20   96-26191   CIP   AC

Maps and graphics supplied by Oxford Cartographers, Oxford, England

Photo research by Matthew Dudley

Cover photo: *Photo Researchers, Inc.*, Rafeal Macia

The photographs in this book are used by permission and through the courtesy of: *Photo Researchers, Inc.*:
Peter Miller, back cover; Rafeal Macia, 6-7; Jim Emmiger, 15; George & Judy Manna, 21; Joe Sohm, 50-51; Jeff
Greenberg dMRp, 71; R.J. Erwin, 123 (top); James Hancock, 123 (bottom); Suzanna L. Collins-The National
Audubon Society Collection, 126. ©*Paul O. Boisvert*: 10-11, 16, 25, 26, 61, 62, 65, 72-73, 75, 81, 82, 89, 90-
91, 107, 109, 110, 119, 128. *The Image Bank*: Michael Melford, 18, 68; Peter Miller, 66, 116; H. Wendler, 83,
87; Frank Whitney, 130; Geoff Gove, 139. *Vermont Dept. of Travel and Tourism*: 23, 79, 84, 104-105, 115.
Courtesy Special Collections, Bailey/Howe Library, University of Vermont: 31, 33 (bottom), 37, 48, 49, 54 (top).
Collection of the New York Historical Society: 35. *Collection of the Vermont Historical Society*: 39, 45, 47 (top and
bottom), 94. *Corbis-Bettmann*: 33 (top), 54 (bottom), 93, 131, 132 (top and bottom), 133, 134, 135, 136 (top
and bottom). *Reuters/Corbis-Bettmann*: 86. *UPI/Corbis-Bettmann*: 55, 97, 101. *Steve Kagen/Gamma Liaison*: 99.
Animals Animals/Margot Conte: 120. *Office of the Secretary of State of Vermont*: 122.

Printed in Italy

3   5   6   4

CONTENTS

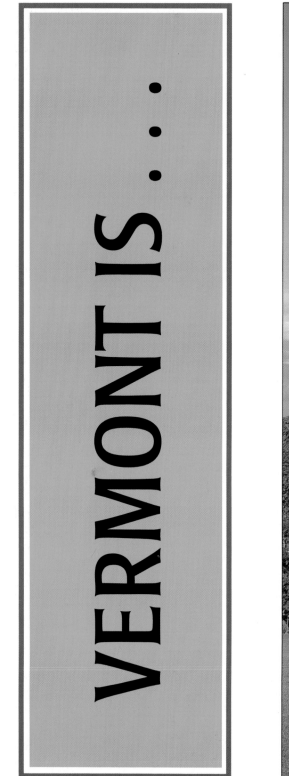

VERMONT IS . . .

Vermont's earliest settlers worked very hard.

"One Morning's Work. Made a fire, mended pants, set the breakfast going, skimmed ten pans of milk, washed the pans, ate breakfast, went to the barn and milked two cows, brought the cream out of the cellar, churned fifteen pounds of butter, made four apple pies, two mince pies, and one custard pie, done up the sink, all done at nine o'clock . . ."

—Mrs. Williamson, age seventy-eight, 1888

The Green Mountain State continues to make great demands upon Vermonters.

"Vermont has a superior quality of life if you don't mind winter."

—journalist Steve Keirnan

"Vermont kids are self-reliant. They know about responsibility and hard work. How to go out and roll up their sleeves and help themselves."

—teacher Charles Gordon

Native Vermonters are often men and women of few words . . .

A woman told Calvin Coolidge, the taciturn thirtieth president who hailed from Vermont, that she bet she could get him to say more than two words. Coolidge thought for a moment and replied: "You lose."

. . . yet they are known for their honesty and neighborliness.

"If the spirit of liberty should vanish in other parts of the Union and support of our institutions should vanish, it could all be replenished by the generous store held by the people of this brave little state of Vermont."   —President Calvin Coolidge

Many people find Vermont the most beautiful state in the union.

"The state remains largely rural, and its only distractions are unsurpassed natural beauty."   —William Corbett, from *Literary New England: A History and Guide*

"If it is not the most beautiful state in the union, which is?"
                                        —Bernard DeVoto, 1954

Most Americans know Vermont as a tiny state in the Northeast that has good skiing, great maple syrup, and beautiful fall foliage—a charming place, far from the problems that plague many communities across the country.

This is only partly true. Vermonters of today are struggling to keep step with the modern world while holding onto the state's classic rural charm. It's a difficult task requiring much thought and work. But then again, overcoming difficulties through hard work is what the native Vermonter is all about.

1 A BEAUTIFUL LAND

The story goes that in 1763, a clergyman named Samuel Peters was standing on top of Killington Mountain in what is now central Vermont. Peters was so overcome by the beautiful scenery that he christened the land with "a name worthy of the Athenians and ancient Spartans . . . in token that her mountains and hills shall be ever green and shall never die."

Peters picked the name "Vert Mont," French for "Green Mountain." Though there are historians who claim that other explorers deserve the credit for the name "Vermont," no one can deny that the name fits. Vermont is, indeed, the Green Mountain State with 420 peaks that run through its middle from Massachusetts all the way to Canada.

What the native Vermonter may not know is that these green mountains, now 3,000 to 4,300 feet, once rose as tall as 15,000 feet—in league with Mount Everest. An ice age changed all that, flattening out the mountains, redirecting ponds, lakes, and rivers, and leaving behind rocks and glacial debris all over the state. The results of this ice age are evident everywhere one looks in Vermont today. It is not at all unusual to find a big boulder smack in the middle of a pasture or a rutted field that slants down and then back up again.

Vermont is located in the part of the United States known as New England. It is a small state. Only New Hampshire, New Jersey,

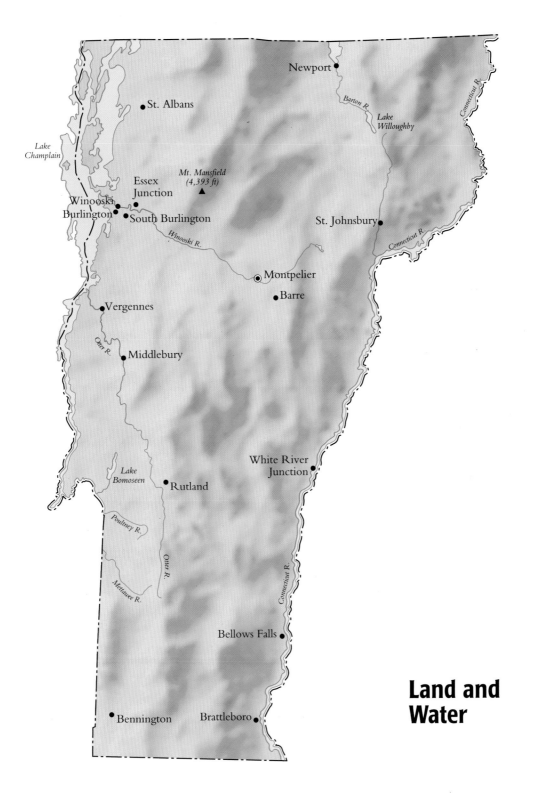

Newport

St. Albans

Barton R.

Lake Champlain

Lake Willoughby

Essex
Junction

*Mt. Mansfield
(4,393 ft)*
▲

Winooski
Burlington
South Burlington

St. Johnsbury

Winooski R.

Connecticut R.

Montpelier

Barre

Vergennes

Otter R.

Middlebury

White River
Junction

*Lake
Bomoseen*

Rutland

Poultney R.

Otter R.

Connecticut R.

Mettawee R.

Bellows Falls

Bennington

Brattleboro

**Land and
Water**

Hawaii, Connecticut, Delaware, and Rhode Island are smaller. Its length north to south is 157.4 miles. Vermont is the only state in this region that does not border the Atlantic Ocean. Its northern neighbor is the Canadian province of Quebec. Massachusetts lies to the south, New York to the west, and New Hampshire to the east.

The Northeast Highlands (usually called the Northeast Kingdom) is a very thinly populated rural area. This deeply wooded part of the state is home to moose, deer, and black bears. Since the soil is poor for farming, logging has been the region's main industry for many years. The Northeast Kingdom borders Canada, and it is not at all unusual to hear French spoken in this part of the state.

The Eastern Foothills lie southwest of the Northeast Kingdom. The land is lower and generally less mountainous than the rest of the state. In the valleys of the foothills there are many dairy farms and apple orchards.

The Mountain Region of Vermont has two chains of peaks. In the southwest, above Brattleboro, is the Taconic Range, Where Mount Equinox and Green Peak are found. Smack down the center of the state are the Green Mountains, including Killington, Ellen, and Camel's Hump, most of which double as ski resorts during the long winter. The Green Mountains make a verdant backbone of the state, which runs unbroken except for two gaps, through which run the Winooski and Lamoille Rivers.

Vermont's longest river, Otter Creek (really more of a ninety-mile stream) runs through the Mountain Region. The state's largest lake, Bomoseen (only four square miles) lies here near Castleton. The highest large body of water, Sterling Pond, lies in this region as well, near Stowe at an elevation of 3,200 feet.

Solitary trout fishing is one of the Green Mountain State's most refreshing joys.

The Vermont Lowlands are in the northwest area of the state. Also known as the Champlain Valley, this region lies along beautiful Lake Champlain and borders the state of New York. Here are many of the state's farms as well as its largest city, Burlington.

THE PEOPLE

As a schoolgirl once put it, "I like Vermont because the trees are close together and the people are far apart." Indeed, Vermont *is* sparsely populated with close to 630,000 people. Assuming

"Vermont's a great place for kids," says resident Frank Buck, "plenty to do in every season."

that the United States has approximately 260 million citizens, Vermonters make up roughly 1/410 of the country.

The population of Vermont is overwhelmingly white and Protestant. In 1970 there were only 761 African Americans living in the entire state. Members of several European groups have immigrated to Vermont, however. In the 1800s Italians came to Vermont to work as masons, and starting around 1850 the Irish came to build railroads and stayed. Vermont's largest population is French Canadian—men and women who have migrated from Quebec and work mostly as loggers in the Northeast Kingdom. Even today, French is the first language of 9 percent of all Vermonters. The latest immigrants to make their way to the Green Mountain State are Latinos, who have settled in very small communities in some of Vermont's cities, notably Rutland.

CLIMATE

Winter is long in Vermont. Anyone thinking of moving there had better come to terms with that fact immediately. Cold winds begin to blow as early as late September, and snowstorms in late April or even early May are not unheard of. In 1816, Vermont settler Francis Hall expressed what generations of visitors have thought ever since: "The thermometer was twenty-two degrees below zero; buffalo hides, bear skins, caps, shawls and handkerchiefs were vainly employed against a degree of cold so much beyond our habits." At times neither buffalo hides nor their modern equivalent, down jackets, can keep the freezing temperatures completely at bay.

After the harsh winter, the Vermonter must suffer through what

Fields lie beneath a thick coat of snow near Jay Peak in March. Spring comes late to Vermont.

is known as "Mud Season," (always capitalized in Vermont) when melting snow turns everything into muck. As one Vermont farmer, Frank Buck of Pittsford, put it: "The mud is everywhere. No matter what you do, you can bet your last dollar that at least once a spring you'll find yourself in muck up to your knees. Not that there *is* much of a spring. It can stay cold until May."

It's often not until Memorial Day that Vermonters can head outside with full confidence that they won't need to bring along a sweater (though it has been known to hail in midsummer). The Vermonter has not yet been born who has not had to shovel his driveway after a blizzard only to find that the car won't start.

The other three seasons in Vermont can be lovely, though. Vermont summers are low on humidity with warm days that rarely seem too hot. Autumn is cool and crisp—perfect sweatshirt or windbreaker weather. As Frank Buck said, of all the seasons in Vermont, spring is the shortest, but perhaps the most welcome after all that snow.

LANDSCAPE

If Vermont has a single defining characteristic it is its astounding natural beauty. When the great ice age passed over the state and then receded, it left a land of hills and valleys. The words "flat" and "straight" simply do not apply to this state and should be duly tucked away until needed to describe states in the Great Plains or Midwest. Vermont is a land of interesting angles. The pastures often climb up and down the sides of hills. Paths through the woods twist through a pine forest or lead unexpectedly to a small pond or meadow. Mountain roads rise and fall, and drivers have to slow down to take hairpin turns.

Though the state has become less dependent on agriculture, the farmhouse still defines the nooks and crannies of this hilly, craggy land. It is nearly impossible to drive down any country road in Vermont and not pass a farm with a herd of cows. Perhaps there's

NO VERMONTERS IN HEAVEN

I dreamed that I went to the City of Gold,
    To Heaven, resplendent and fair,
And after I entered the beautiful fold,
    By one in authority there I was told
That not a Vermonter was there.

"Impossible, sir, for from my own town
    Many sought this delectable place,
And each must be here, with a harp or a crown,
And a conqueror's palm and a clean linen gown,
    Received through unmerited grace."

The angel replied: "All Vermonters come here
    When they first depart from the earth,
But after a day or a month or a year,
They restless and lonesome and homesick appear,
    And sigh for the land of their birth.

"They tell of ravines, wild, secluded and deep,
    And flower-decked landscapes serene,
Of towering mountains, imposing and steep,
Adown which the torrents exultantly leap,
    Through forests perennially green.

"We give them the best that the kingdom provides
    They have everything here that they want,
But not a Vermonter in Heaven abides:
A very brief period here he resides,
    Then hikes his way back to Vermont."
           —Author unknown

a small pond nearby and a few horses or sheep. Or maybe there's a pasture with bales of hay stacked in the middle. And surrounding these farms are wooded mountains good for hiking in the summer and skiing in the winter.

Of course, there are towns, too. But most are still organized around a single main street, complete with several church spires and a general store. Most towns have only one movie theater, which shows only one movie at a time. Even in Burlington, the state's

"Vermont is behind everybody's time—the reason so many people love it," claims Vermonter Rickey Gard Diamond. "Who doesn't like to go back for a visit to simpler, quieter places?"

largest city, (though not a "city" at all by the standards of some-one from Boston or New York) the main shopping district is centered on several avenues that are closed off from cars.

The look of Vermont distinguishes it as a throwback to a bygone, simpler time. Vermont is the home of stone fences, covered bridges, red farmhouses—everything that might be considered quaint. Perhaps that is why journalist Neal R. Peirce wrote: "Vermont is perhaps the only place in America that a stranger can feel homesick for before he has even left it." Or as novelist Sinclair Lewis wrote in 1929:

> I like Vermont because it is quiet, because you have a population that is solid and not driven mad by the American mania—that mania which considers a town of 4,000 twice as good as a town of 2,000, or a city of 100,000, fifty times as good as a town of 2,000. Following that reasoning, one would get the charming paradox that Chicago would be ten times better than the entire state of Vermont, but I have been in Chicago, and have not found it so.

The landscape of Vermont reminds visitors of America as they imagine it was two hundred years ago. For that reason, Vermont's economy has come to rely more and more on tourism. Every year people from the cities to the south, notably New York, journey to Vermont to breathe the fresh air and take in the lovely scenery.

THE BEAUTY OF THE SEASONS

In autumn the state is at its prettiest. As author Henry James wrote in 1907: "A solitary maple on a woodside flames in single scarlet,

STONE WALLS

When the last glacier melted away about 25,000 years ago, it left thousands of granite stones strewn all over the Vermont landscape. Leave it to Vermonters to find a good use for all those stray rocks.

From 1700 to 1850, early settlers used the pieces of granite to build stone walls to mark boundaries between farms and pastures. The bigger rocks were placed on the ground, the smaller rocks on top. Often the larger stones were set in a trench to create a strong foundation. It was not easy work. Stone-wall building required a good deal of skill and remains an artistic craft that is passed down through the generations.

One of the most enduring and charming parts of the Vermont landscape, stone walls still divide pastures and ramble along country roads. They curve around hills and dip and rise through valleys—a reminder of the brave settlers who first tamed this rocky terrain.

recalls nothing so much as the daughter of a noble house dressed for a fancy ball, with the whole family gathered round to admire her before she goes." Another American man of letters, Henry David Thoreau, put it this way: "All the hills blush; I think that autumn must be the best season to journey over even the Green Mountains. You frequently exclaim to yourself, what *red* maples!"

At its peak the foliage can be awe inspiring. Imagine hiking to the top of one of Vermont's many tall peaks and looking out as far as you can see over a sea of bright colors. Of course, you don't have to climb a mountain to experience autumn in Vermont. A short bike ride, a walk to the post office, even a step outside to bring in the morning paper gives most Vermonters enough to look at to last the average foliage-starved city dweller for years.

Autumn isn't the only time Vermont shows off its immense beauty. Snow covers the state for a good five months of the year, blanketing everything in white. (The skiers who come to the state in droves find this sight especially beautiful.) Spring brings new flowers—aster, cattail, gentian, jack-in-the-pulpit, to name a few—and the return of leaves to the trees. Farmers plant for the next season. In summer sailboats dot Vermont's many lakes, and hikers wind their way along its mountainous paths.

What remains in all seasons is a rural charm unmatched anywhere else in the country. As Sinclair Lewis said in 1929: "It is hard in this day, in which the American tempo is so speeded up, to sit back and be satisfied with what you have. It requires education and culture to appreciate a quiet place, but any fool can appreciate noise. . . . [Other states] were ruined by that mania. It must not happen in Vermont.

Three boys in Vergennes get ready for some autumn fun, romping in fallen leaves.

Vermont is filled with many back roads, perfect for an afternoon ride.

ENVIRONMENTAL CONCERNS

For the most part, Vermont has heeded Lewis's warning and remains a quiet place, blessed with enormous natural beauty. In 1970, the state took a big step toward preserving its identity when Vermonters passed a revolutionary law called Act 250. This ruling put a stop to uncontrolled housing and business development. Permits are now required "for any substantial development, public or private." In other words, every time someone wants to build a house or a store or engage in any kind of construction, the state considers a series of questions before it gives permission: Will air and water be polluted? Will a strain be put on existing water supplies? Can roads handle increased traffic? Can schools accommodate an increased population? Will the natural beauty of the state and its wildlife be abused?

Vermont is the first and only state in the nation to pass such sweeping legislation to protect its natural heritage. Though Act 250 is now a hard-and-fast part of the state law, it is not without its detractors. Some people believe that the law has slowed down the rate of the state's industrial expansion. There have been cases of businesses taking their jobs elsewhere rather than deal with the stringent guidelines of Vermont's environmental laws.

Vermont legislators knew what they were getting into, however. As other states become more suburban and industrialized, Vermont is struggling to keep its unique character. It's an uphill battle, but thus far Vermont has managed to hold onto its identity as a rural state, comprised of small, close-knit communities.

2 AN INDEPENDENT HERITAGE

The Connecticut River at Barnet, Vermont, *by Robert Huntoon.*

To most Americans, Vermont history begins and ends with Ethan Allen and the Green Mountain Boys. Allen, who was instrumental in helping Vermont reach statehood around the time of the American Revolution, has nearly attained the stature of a tall-tale hero. According to Vermont myth, Allen could shoot a grizzly between the eyes from a distance of two hundred yards, wrestle a panther to the ground, and chew iron nails to little bits.

Despite Allen's heroics, both real and imaginary, it is very true that Vermont does not figure prominently in the overall picture of American history. Only two presidents, Chester A. Arthur and Calvin Coolidge, hailed from Vermont, and both of their tenures in the White House are considered to be unremarkable. Only one battle in the American Revolution was fought on Vermont soil, and none in the Civil War . No famous inventors or scientists have hailed from the Green Mountain State. In fact, Vermont has often bent over backwards to go against the flow of the country. It was one of only two states to vote against Franklin Roosevelt in 1936. During the American Revolution, many Vermonters didn't even want to be part of the colonies, and some of the colonies wanted nothing to do with Vermont!

Even so, the Green Mountain State has a special and interesting history. Vermont's proud and stubborn people have made certain of that.

The Abenaki were among the first Vermonters to go maple sugaring. Here, a group of Abenaki women boil down buckets of maple sap while men plant corn in the fields.

EARLIEST SETTLERS

Paleo-Indians may have lived in the region as much as ten thousand years ago, but it isn't until about the year A. D. 1300 that Vermont history begins to be recorded. At this time a Native American tribe, the Abenaki, settled in small villages around the large lake they called Petoubouque, which is now called Lake Champlain. These people lived a simple life. In the spring they planted corn and squash. In the summer they hunted deer, squirrel, and bear. They also fished the many streams and the large lake. During winter the tribe survived on what it had been able to grow and save from the warmer months.

Though essentially a peaceful tribe, the Abenaki had an enemy—the Iroquois—who lived on the western side of the large lake. For many years the two tribes feuded and fought over land.

SAMUEL DE CHAMPLAIN

In 1609 a French explorer named Samuel de Champlain sailed into Lake Petoubouque. (Champlain named the lake after himself in keeping with the custom of many white explorers.) Champlain and his men instantly found themselves in a battle with a band of Iroquois. This pleased the Abenaki enormously, and they persuaded Champlain to attack the Iroquois a second time. Needless to say, the Iroquois did not take kindly to such treatment. When other French settlers arrived, they constructed forts to guard against future Iroquois raids. Fort Saint Anne was the first, built in 1666 on an island in Lake Champlain.

THE FRENCH AND INDIAN WARS

During this same period, the British were colonizing the so-called New World. Just south of Vermont were the English colonies of Massachusetts, New York, and New Hampshire. The English claims didn't stop there, however. Eager for more land, they joined the Iroquois and set their sights on Vermont. The French turned to the Abenaki and fought back. After nine years of fighting (from 1754 to 1763), the British drove the French settlers and most of the Abenaki out of the Champlain Valley. This ended what came to be known as the French and Indian Wars and left Vermont in the hands of the British.

Samuel de Champlain, the first European to set foot in Vermont

Lake Champlain during the time of the Abenaki. Indian myth says that Vermont's largest lake was formed by a creator named Odzihozo. When the lake was finished, Odzihozo then transformed himself into a rock on Burlington Bay so he could enjoy the spectacular view for all eternity.

WHO WAS JOHNE GRAYE?

Was Samuel de Champlain actually the first European to see the state of Vermont? It isn't exactly clear. In 1853, in Swanton, Vermont, two workmen found a lead tube. Inside the tube they found a message dated November 29, 1564:

> *This is the solme daye*
> *I must now die this is*
> *the 90th day sine we*
> *lef the Ship all have*
> *Perished and on the*
>
> *Banks of this river*
> *I die to (or, so) farewelle*
> *may future Posteritye*
> *knowe our end*

Who was this mysterious man and what was his expedition? The truth of the matter is that no one really knows. Even so, this note excited the imaginations of Vermonters for years. Perhaps Champlain wasn't the first European to bask in the glory of the Green Mountains?

Today, however, most historians think the note to be a hoax. There is no supporting evidence that there were expeditions by white men to Vermont in 1564. Also, a Harvard professor, Samuel Eliot Morrison, put the document through a handwriting and ink analysis and declared it fraudulent.

Was Johne Graye a real person or the creation of a Vermonter with a lively sense of humor? Any further investigation is limited by the fact that both the note and the pipe have been lost!

THE GRANTS

Even before the British had driven the French out of Vermont, governors of New Hampshire and New York were busy claiming portions of what is now Vermont. Unfortunately, the two states

The Champlain Valley was the scene of fighting among the British, the French, and the Abenaki.

often laid claim to the same land. It seemed that everyone wanted a piece of Vermont.

By the early 1760s New Hampshire governor Benning Wentworth was granting land in Vermont like it was going out of style. In fact, he sold so many acres that the land began to be called the "Hampshire Grants" and the people who lived there "the Grants."

The people of New York—the Yorkers—were not pleased. After all, they had claimed Vermont as their own. Soon the Yorkers began to charge the people of the Grants rent for the right to live on their claims. Obviously, the Grants didn't like this idea at all. Why should they pay rent on land they had already purchased under the authority of the New Hampshire governor?

The problem seemed to be resolved in 1767 when the king of England ordered that the Yorkers not bother the New Hampshire-men already settled in Vermont. But by 1769 the Yorkers couldn't bear to watch what they felt was their land being taken over, and they demanded that Vermont be put under their complete control. Tensions were boiling over.

ETHAN ALLEN AND THE GREEN MOUNTAIN BOYS

This is where Ethan Allen enters the story. As the Yorkers grew testier, Ethan was called upon by the Grants to help protect them and to bring their case to the courts.

The first thing Allen did was obtain documents supporting the Hampshire Grants. But a judge in Albany, New York (a Yorker through and through), would not recognize the New Hampshire deeds as valid.

The story goes that Allen retired to a local tavern, where he was approached by two New York lawyers. Apparently the lawyers offered a bribe: They would make it worth Allen's while if he could persuade his New Hampshire friends to recognize New York's authority. Allen would have none of it and replied: "The gods of the hills are not the gods of the valleys." Though this quote is one of the most famous in Vermont's history, its literal meaning is unclear. What *is* clear is that Allen refused the New York bribe and returned to Bennington where, along with his younger brother, Ira, he organized a band of two hundred men to protect the Grants from the Yorkers. Ethan and Ira named them "the Green Mountain Boys."

Perhaps Ethan Allen couldn't wrestle a panther to the ground or chew nails to bits, but he and his brother certainly knew how to make life miserable for any Yorkers who dared settle in Vermont. In 1771, the Allens and their crew told a New York surveyor to leave the state or be murdered. Later that year, the Green Mountain Boys burned the cabins and fields of a group of Scots with New York titles. Allen's men whipped Yorker officials with sticks and once used ropes to lift a prominent Yorker in a chair and left him to dangle over a tavern for several hours.

The Allens became so notorious the New York Assembly passed the Outlawry Act, which called for the Green Mountain Boys—who they called "abominable wretches, rioters and traitors"—to surrender in seventy days or be shot. Ethan Allen simply renamed the law "the Bloody Act" and continued doing what he had done all along: protect the Grants.

Ethan Allen and his Green Mountain Boys teach a Yorker a lesson. In 1781, Allen wrote: "I am as determined to preserve the Independence of Vermont as Congress is that of the Union and rather than fail I will retire with my hardy green mountain boys into the caverns of the mountains and make war on all mankind."

THE CATAMOUNT—SYMBOL OF THE STATE

Back in the days of Ethan Allen, catamounts (more commonly known as panthers) roamed the woods of Vermont. When the Green Mountain Boys formed to protect the Grants from the Yorkers, the first act of the band was to place a stuffed catamount on top of a tavern in Bennington, Vermont, facing New York.

The panther plays a central role in Vermont mythology. Just as tall tales came to be told of Ethan Allen, tales were told of these mighty cats who would strike and kill at will. The cat was strong and proud, able to take care of itself. So was the Vermonter.

Even though the last known catamount in the state was killed in 1881 (its stuffed body may be viewed at the Vermont Historical Society), the mystique of the panther remains strong in Vermont. In fact, there are Vermonters to this day who claim that they've seen a panther in the woods, even though the animal always seems to disappear before it can be photographed.

THE AMERICAN REVOLUTION

As the Green Mountain Boys continued to fight for Vermont, the first thirteen colonies, including New York and New Hampshire, declared a war of revolution against Britain.

The Grants were suddenly put in a strange spot. Their interests were more aligned with Britain than with the colonies. After all, it was the Yorkers, not King George, who wanted to take over their lands. But Allen would not join British forces, saying he would never agree to any "plan to sell his country and his honor by

With the help of his brother Ira and Benedict Arnold (later an infamous traitor), Ethan Allen took Fort Ticonderoga from the British.

betraying the trust reposed to him." In that spirit, Ethan Allen and his band raided Fort Ticonderoga, a British outpost on the western shores of Lake Champlain in 1775. Allen cited his "sincere passion for liberty" to explain his sudden decision to take on the English.

But Allen's and the Grants' allegiance to the colonies stopped there. As the war raged to the south, the British did their best to bring Vermont over to their side, arguing that New York and the

THE RIFLEMEN OF BENNINGTON

On August 13, 1777, a force of about 1,200 British and Hessian soldiers attacked Bennington in hopes of finding food and ammunition. They were surprised and defeated in the Battle of Bennington by the Green Mountain Boys under the leadership of General John Stark. This battle was a turning point in the Revolutionary War.

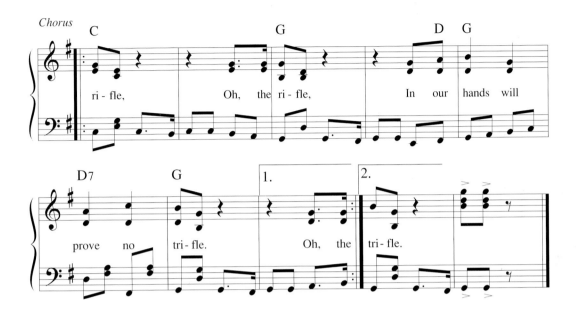

Ye ride a goodly steed, ye may know another master,
Ye forward come with speed, but ye'll learn to back much faster
When you meet our mountain boys and their leader Johnny Stark
Lads who make but little noise, lads who always hit the mark. *Chorus*

Had ye no graves at home, across the briny water,
That hither ye must come, like bullocks to the slaughter?
Well, if we work must do, why, the sooner 'tis begun,
If flint and powder hold but true, the sooner 'twill be done. *Chorus*

Continental Congress would never recognize Vermont's claims. In fact, there were rumors that New York and New Hampshire were already discussing how they would split Vermont between them after the war. If Vermont fought with the British and won, the Grants could have the status of a separate province. Allen even wrote a letter to the young United States Continental Congress in 1781, which stated:

> I am as determined to preserve the Independence of Vermont as Congress is that of the Union and rather than fail I will retire with my hardy green mountain boys into the caverns of the mountains and make war on all mankind.

When all was said and done, Allen and the Grants spent much of the war neutral. (Allen also spent a good three years of the war in an English prison!) When the colonies won the war, Vermont was finally admitted as the fourteenth state, agreeing to pay New York $30,000 as compensation for any past claims.

The road to Vermont's ultimate inclusion in the United States was certainly not smooth. As Nicholas Muller III, an early Vermont historian, once wrote:

> Conceived in a bewildering mix of geographic ignorance, conflicting and even larcenous land claims, and the reckless ambitions of colonial land speculators, Vermont was finally born in the swirling confusion of complex local, national and international events.

FAST GROWTH

During the early years of America, Vermont was the fastest growing state in the nation. From 1790 to 1800, the Green Mountain

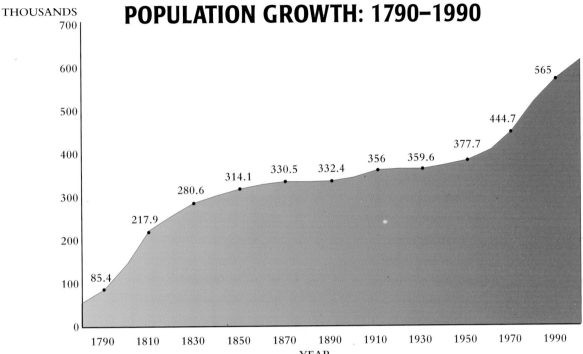

POPULATION GROWTH: 1790–1990

THOUSANDS

State's population doubled. For a while, Vermont was the place to be, especially for the young. The majority of the people were under twenty-six years old.

Land was cheap, resources seemed infinite, and industries were expanding: sawmills and lumberyards in particular. Farmers chopped down trees and made potash—an ash used in soap and fertilizer. Unfortunately, two thousand pounds of wood were needed to make just seven pounds of potash. By the early 1800s much of the land was treeless.

In the following years, Vermont quickly depleted many of its natural resources. Its timber was pretty much gone by 1830. Fish in some of its streams were scarce. Otter Creek (which still runs through the heart of Vermont) hadn't seen an actual otter since 1820.

REGROUPING

Yet all was certainly not lost for Vermont. Resourceful to the end, Vermonters turned to other industries and did their best to scrape together a living. During the War of 1812—another dispute between the young United States and the British—wool was in high demand, and a sheep craze hit the state. In modern times it is often said that Vermont has more cows than people. But in 1840, the small state had six sheep for every person! Lewis Stilwell of Dartmouth College got it right when he wrote: "Not even the lower South in the heyday of 'King Cotton,' was more thoroughly committed to a single crop than was the Vermont of the 30s." But in the 1850s things changed. The price of wool dropped dramatically, and farmers quickly sold off their flocks.

Meanwhile, other industries began to flourish. In the 1830s Windsor, Vermont, became a leader in the manufacture of machine tools, such as lathes, drills, and planters. The 1850s brought a wave of Irish immigrants to the state to build railroads.

Despite the Vermonters' ability to switch to new industries, many natives began to leave the state in search of greater opportunity elsewhere. Vermont may have been beautiful, but many people found its rocky soil and mountainous terrain quite limiting, both

"Not even the lower South in the heyday of 'King Cotton' was more thoroughly committed to a single crop [sheep] than was the Vermont of the [18] 30's."
—Lewis Stilwell, Dartmouth College

financially and emotionally. As a Vermont girl, Sally Rice, put it in 1839: "I can never be happy there among so many mountains." Like many other natives, Sally Rice moved to Connecticut to work in a textile mill.

THE CIVIL WAR AND BEYOND

The Vermonters who remained loyal to the state were men and women of strong moral beliefs. In 1852, when residents realized that drinking had become a serious problem, Vermont followed Maine in prohibiting liquor. Vermonters were also morally opposed to slavery. By the end of the 1830s Vermont was one of the most abolitionist states in the Union (abolitionists were men and women who fought to end slavery). Many Vermont boys signed up with the Union army as soon as the Civil War broke out.

After the war, more industry came to Vermont. Masons from Italy came to carve marble found in Vermont's quarries. The town of Barre became a center of the American granite industry. French Canadians immigrated to the Northeast Kingdom to·work in lumberyards. Vermont also turned from sheep to cows and soon became the largest dairy producing state in the nation. From the late 1800s until 1963 the old adage was true: Vermont really did have more cows than people.

THE TWENTIETH CENTURY

Though Vermont has continued to lose population, those people who have stayed are proud of their state. Its granite and lumber industries contributed greatly to World War II (not to mention the fifty thousand Vermont boys who proudly marched off to battle). Earlier, during the Great Depression of the 1930s, out-of-work Vermonters paved roads and worked on flood-control projects. But many Vermonters weren't as affected by the nation's economic collapse as other Americans. After all, it had always been tough to make a living in this beautiful but craggy state.

Today, only one of twenty-five Vermonters work in agriculture. The rest work in manufacturing or service jobs. Though the state

A typical Vermont scene—cows waiting to be milked. By 1930, a higher percentage of Vermonters depended on dairy farming for a living than did the citizens of any other state.

In 1869, one hundred farmers gathered at the Montpelier state-house and founded the first statewide dairy association. Dairy farming soon became big business in the Green Mountain State.

Workers at Proctor Marble often used Danby marble, still favored by architects around the country for its strength and beauty.

still has some difficulty attracting big businesses, Vermonters, like the generations before them, have become adept at getting by on what they have. Tourism, some farming, and manufacturing keep the people afloat. Vermonters may not be as rich as the people of other states with greater natural resources and more agreeable soil, but they remain a proud breed, willing to work hard to carve out a better future.

Six "flatlanders"—early tourists—enjoy the Vermont scenery. Matthew H. Buckham, president of Vermont University, expressed the sentiments of many Vermonters when he said in 1867: "Let us do all we can to keep up the notion among our city cousins, that to live 'away up in Vermont,' is the American equivalent for being exiled to Siberia."

3 EVERYONE HAS A SAY

The state capitol in Montpelier

Vermont remains a state of small towns—towns where everyone goes to the same schools and shops at the same stores, where you might run into your state legislator at the general store on Main Street and talk about the weather and ask after each other's family. It's also a place where each citizen has a unique opportunity to participate in major decisions. As many a native has said: "Hands-on governing is what Vermont is all about."

INSIDE GOVERNMENT

Vermont's government is divided into three branches: executive, legislative, and judicial. But in Vermont, many economic decisions are made at local town meetings. In these meetings, a single citizen can make his or her voice clearly heard.

Executive. The governor is the chief executive officer of the state. In Vermont, the governor is elected to a two-year term with no term limits. The chief executive appoints judges as well as up to one thousand employees of various agencies. The governor is responsible for the state budget and can veto measures submitted by the legislature.

Vermont's greatest governor may well have been Thomas Chittenden, who served for eighteen years (1778–1789 and 1790–1797). A tavern keeper with only one eye, Chittenden served

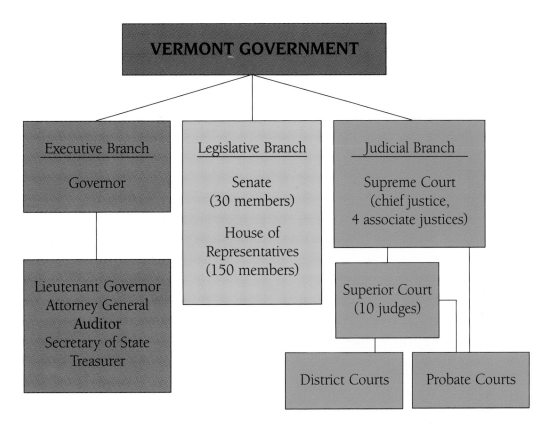

VERMONT GOVERNMENT

Executive Branch

Governor

Lieutenant Governor
Attorney General
Auditor
Secretary of State
Treasurer

Legislative Branch

Senate
(30 members)

House of
Representatives
(150 members)

Judicial Branch

Supreme Court
(chief justice,
4 associate justices)

Superior Court
(10 judges)

District Courts

Probate Courts

through Vermont's turbulent era as an independent republic until 1791 and helped guide the land to statehood. Chittenden's reelection record is unique in a state that has been historically stingy about giving its governors more than one term. A list of Vermont chief executives is long—most were granted only two years to prove themselves, then voted out of office.

One of Vermont's most popular political figures of the last fifty years has been George Aiken. Governor for two terms from 1937 to 1941, Aiken later served in the Senate and was one of the first senators to question the United States' policy on Vietnam, declaring: "[We should] declare victory and get out."

In 1985, the Green Mountain State elected Madeleine Kunin governor. The first woman and Jewish person to inhabit the office,

Thomas Chittenden, Vermont's first governor. The epitaph on his gravestone reads: "Out of storm and manifold perils rose an enduring state, the home of freedom and unity." The phrase "freedom and unity" is the state's official motto.

Senator George D. Aiken, sawing wood in Putney on his eightieth birthday. A hardworking Vermont native, Aiken was known for spending no more than twenty dollars on each of his many reelection campaigns.

Kunin, a Democrat, became a great advocate for women's rights and went on to serve in President Bill Clinton's Department of Education.

Governor Richard Snelling, a Republican, was elected to two terms—first in 1977, then, after losing to Kunin in 1985, he got back to the statehouse in 1991. Snelling understood the need to keep the state's books in order and was on his way to balancing the state budget when he died in office. Picking up the reins of government in 1991 was Howard Dean. A doctor by profession, Dean continued to fight for a balanced budget and became a champion of health-care reform.

Governor Madeleine Kunin addressing the Democratic Convention in 1988.

DOCTOR GOVERNOR

Howard Dean became a member of the Vermont House of Representatives in 1983. Like most Vermont state representatives, Dean kept his day job: a full-time doctor in Burlington. But Dean was destined for more than medicine. He was elected lieutenant governor in 1986 and reelected in 1988. In 1990 when Governor Richard A. Snelling died suddenly in office, Dean took over the top spot. Appropriately, Dean was informed that he was to be the Green Mountain State's next governor while seeing a patient.

Dean has championed a variety of causes in his career in Vermont politics. While in the state legislature, he founded the Vermont Youth Conservation Corps and co-chaired the Long Trail Protection Fund. While lieutenant governor, Dean was especially interested in children's issues.

As governor of the state, Dean has focused on health issues, rewriting some of Vermont's health-insurance laws. His welfare bill emphasizes job training and requires all recipients of public assistance to work after a certain period of time. Dean has also been grappling with one of Vermont's most difficult problems: a state budget deficit of $64 million.

Though Dean certainly hasn't solved all of Vermont's problems, he's out there fighting for the state every day. And most Vermonters seem to approve of the job he's doing: he won election in 1994 with nearly 70 percent of the vote.

Legislative. The legislature is the lawmaking branch of state government. Like most other states, Vermont's is made up of two houses: a 30-member senate and a 150-member house of representatives. The legislators can pass a law by a simple majority vote in both houses. They can override a governor's veto with a two-thirds vote. Both senators and representatives are elected to a two-year term. There are no term limits in Vermont. In fact, a recent bill before the legislature called for stretching the terms of the governor, senators, and legislators to four years.

As of late, Vermont's legislature has its work cut out for it. The Vermont tax rate is high. As D. K. Smith, former chairman of Middlebury College's economics department notes: "People who come to Vermont have got to love it [because] 37 to 38 percent of their income is taxed."

Though it may sound a bit dull, the words "property tax" are enough to make many a Vermonter's blood boil. All public schools in the state are funded by property taxes. But there are some glaring inequities. The people lucky enough to live in richer towns don't have to pay as much out of their own pocket to fund their schools. The businesses in their towns (the ski resorts, for example) shoulder much of the tax burden. But those Vermonters who live in poorer areas aren't as lucky. They have to dig deeply into their own pockets to support their schools. As one old native declared, "Why should I pay good money out of my thin wallet when a flatlander with a thick wallet laughs all the way to the bank?"

Many solutions have been dangled before the legislature. Some say there should be statewide property assessment and taxes. This would even out the tax among the richer and poorer towns. Others favor a homestead exemption, which would allow those in poorer towns to pay less. Still others favor raising the state income tax. Nothing has been decided yet, but sharing the educational burden is a problem that is still under heated discussion.

The legislature has also been looking for creative ways to balance the state budget. Once again, the solutions boil down to different approaches to the old taxation game. Some suggest letting the towns collect taxes in new ways. Some call for a gasoline tax or raising the tax on second homes. Of course, all these solutions have fervent supporters and equally fervent detractors. As Steve Spensley, a fifth-grade teacher from Pittsford, observes, many poor Vermonters "want to stick it to" the wealthy out-of-staters who enjoy the state's glorious scenery but whose property taxes are generally low. (Vacation homes are not taxed as highly as primary residences).

One of Vermont's greatest challenges in the years ahead is to balance the state budget and distribute the state tax burden fairly.

Judiciary. Each of Vermont's fourteen counties has a family court, where divorces and child custody cases are decided, a district court for criminal cases, and a superior court for civil law suits. The judges who preside over these courts are elected by the state legislature every six years. Each of Vermont's counties also has at least one probate court that presides over cases involving wills, adoptions, and guardianships. These probate judges are elected to a four-year term. Vermont also has a supreme court with five judges appointed by the governor to decided cases appealed in the lower courts.

An interesting wrinkle on Vermont's judicial landscape is that two assistant judges are also elected in each county. Before the American Revolution, the king of England appointed judges to oversee each county. Two assistant judges, who didn't have to be lawyers, were then elected within each community to help the king's judge. As in days past, Vermont's assistant judges don't have to have any legal training whatsoever. In fact, many assistant judges are simply retired men or women. Though they may know absolutely nothing about the law, their fellow citizens are trusting them to put their common sense to work in deciding cases.

The Vermont Constitution states that all judges must retire at age seventy. Although there have been several lawsuits brought by elderly judges who weren't yet ready to hang up their robes, the Vermont courts have always stuck by their constitution. Apparently the Green Mountain State's founding fathers didn't want to take a chance on the judgment of a judge a bit on in years. Whether that is fair or not, that's the way it is in Vermont.

THE TOWN MEETING

There are 251 towns in Vermont—at least half with under five hundred citizens—and each person is given a significant say in how their money is spent. Allocating funds for everything from fire trucks to schools is decided on the town level.

Once a week each town has a meeting to discuss and vote on various issues concerning their community. There is no elected official who runs these gatherings. Rather, at the end of one week's discussion someone might volunteer to moderate the coming session.

Most out-of-staters probably imagine the town meeting to be a quaint and polite tradition from yesteryear. That is not usually the case. Town meetings are often contentious. People generally have strong opinions where their pocketbook is concerned. No one wants their taxes raised to support projects they find unnecessary. In a big city such as New York it is often difficult to see where one's money is going. In a small town in Vermont, however, citizens can see their tax dollars at work every time they step out the door. Because Vermonters don't often have enormous wealth, people will argue for hours to keep costs down. As Steven Keirnan, an editor of the *Burlington Free Press,* says: "People feel like they own their state."

Once, the town of Arlington debated whether their tax dollars should go toward repairing bridges or building a new elementary school. After listening quietly for a while, Patrick Thompson, the village grocer, rose to his feet and declared:

> I say "If we have to choose, let the bridges fall down!" What kind of a town would we rather have, fifty years from now—a place where nit-wit folks go back and forth over good bridges? Or a town which has always given its children a fair chance, and prepares them to hold their own in modern life? If they've had a fair chance, they can build their own bridges.

Thompson's speech swayed his fellow citizens, and the money was voted to the school.

The advantage of a government that allows so much direct participation is that each town has direct control over what it wants. If a town wants to spend ten thousand dollars on a new road grader, it can get it done. If it thinks it needs another policeman patrolling Main Street, it can decide the matter for itself. But a price is paid in waste. It costs a lot for every town to have its own fire department, police department, and school. For that reason, some Vermont towns have begun merging fire departments and schools.

A town meeting in Waterville. Many of Vermont's most important economic issues are decided by ordinary citizens at their local town hall or school.

Some might argue that paying a higher price is worth the luxury of local control. Others would prefer to share their authority with another couple of towns and save money.

Though the debates can rage, it is rare that the enmity spills over to day-to-day life. Once the meeting is over, most Vermonters successfully convert back to good neighbors. It is not at all unusual for two people to argue heatedly over whether to repave Main Street then to sit down to a chicken dinner afterwards, still the best of friends.

THE RIGHT TO BEAR ARMS

Vermont is a state that believes strongly in the Second Amendment, which gives every citizen the right to bear arms. The state's many pastures, woods, and mountains provide excellent deer hunting. Many natives are taught how to use guns at an early age.

Largely devoid of the serious crime that plagues many big cities, most Vermonters feel comfortable owning guns. The old adage that "guns don't kill, people do" seems to hold true in Vermont. The murder rate is extraordinarily low; there were only five reported homicides in 1994 throughout the entire state. Even Bernie Sanders, the state's socialist legislator who now serves in the United States House of Representatives is against gun control. In 1990, the enormous and powerful NRA (National Rifle Association) fought the candidacy of Peter Smith, a moderate Republican

Hunting remains a popular pastime in the Green Mountain State.

who took a stand against some of the lobby's more extreme positions. It didn't take long for bumper stickers to appear, reading: "Smith & Wesson, Yes. Peter Smith, No." The clear implication to any native Vermonter was that, if elected, Peter Smith would take away their guns. Though that wasn't true, the damage was done, and Smith, a man whose other political beliefs were in line with the majority of the state, lost the election.

CRIME AND DRUGS

Due to Vermont's rural character, many of the problems associated with big cities haven't made their way into its culture. When George Aiken was governor in the 1930s and early 1940s, a window in the statehouse was kept open so he could sneak into his office at night when he forgot his keys. "The Aiken Window" remained an entryway into the statehouse until the late 1960s and was used by the governor, state employees, and the press.

Unfortunately, those days have passed. Today, the statehouse has an electronic monitoring system and televised surveillance of visitors. Still, Vermont remains an extremely safe place and was recently ranked the safest state in the country in which to live. There are some causes for concern as Vermonters look toward the twenty-first century, however. In August 1995, Vermont's first gang-related violence broke out in Rutland when a group of Latino teenagers who had recently moved there fought with a group of local whites. Though no one was hurt, the incident registered deeply with Vermonters, who thought they would spend their lives reading about such episodes in out-of-state papers rather than in

TEN LARGEST CITIES

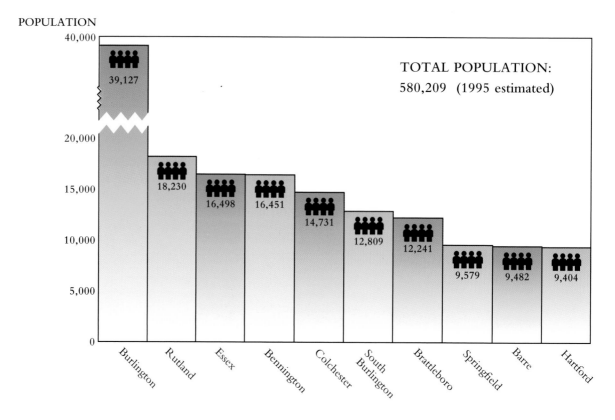

POPULATION

40,000

TOTAL POPULATION:
580,209 (1995 estimated)

39,127

20,000

18,230

15,000

16,498   16,451

14,731

10,000

12,809

12,241

9,579   9,482   9,404

5,000

0

Burlington   Rutland   Essex   Bennington   Colchester   South Burlington   Brattleboro   Springfield   Barre   Hartford

their own. As Ron Powers, a Pulitzer Prize-winning journalist who teaches at Middlebury College, observed: "Until the Rutland gangs, Vermonters comforted themselves by saying the worst of the 20th century would never get here."

Though drugs aren't a major problem in Vermont, the state is concerned enough to have set up a help line for those who might have a cocaine problem. Alcohol remains the most abused drug in the state, especially among teenagers. Alcohol-awareness seminars are now held in many Vermont high schools.

Most Vermonters find it hard to imagine big city problems invading their quiet communities.

THE ECONOMY

Traditionally Vermont's economy has depended upon manufacturing and agriculture. But times have definitely begun to change in the Green Mountain State.

The state still enjoys a high number of cows, but more of them are now owned by fewer people. As it has become harder and harder for dairy farmers to make a living, many have had to get out of the business, selling off their farms to larger and wealthier rivals. And what are these ex-farmers doing? They are mostly turning to service jobs, working in stores or fast-food restaurants.

Farms cover more than one-fifth of the Green Mountain State, but only one out of twenty-five Vermonters still works in agriculture or dairy farming.

Changing times have brought great advances to manufacturing across the nation. Some of Vermont's businesses have found it hard to keep up. There are pockets of extreme poverty in Vermont not usually seen by the out-of-state leaf peeper. One of ten Vermonters receives food stamps. About a third of the state budget goes to welfare.

Act 250. Act 250 (the law that requires each new business in Vermont to pass a series of environmental tests) hasn't made it easier for Vermont's economy to remain strong. D. K. Smith of Middlebury put it this way: "Act 250 is good for those of us who have ways of earning a living."

Many Vermonters want to keep out of the kind of big business that could greatly mar Vermont's heritage. In recent years, CNS

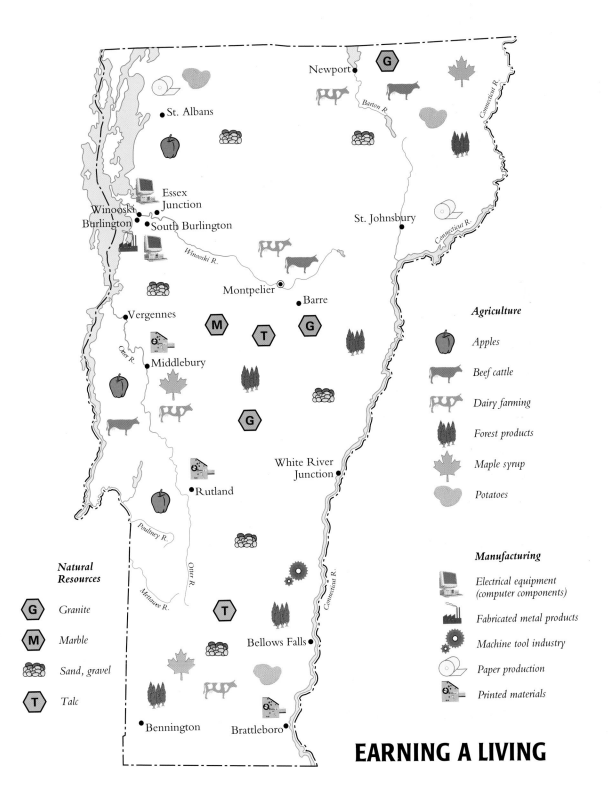

Newport

St. Albans

Essex
Junction

Winooski
Burlington
South Burlington

Winooski R.

St. Johnsbury

Montpelier

Barre

Vergennes

Otter R.

Middlebury

White River
Junction

Rutland

Poultney R.

Otter R.

Battawee R.

Bellows Falls

Bennington

Brattleboro

Barton R.

Connecticut R.

Connecticut R.

Connecticut R.

Agriculture

Apples

Beef cattle

Dairy farming

Forest products

Maple syrup

Potatoes

Manufacturing

Electrical equipment
(computer components)

Fabricated metal products

Machine tool industry

Paper production

Printed materials

**Natural
Resources**

G Granite

M Marble

Sand, gravel

T Talc

EARNING A LIVING

One of Barre's great granite quarries

Whole Groceries, the largest wholesale grocer in the state, tried to get permission to build a new warehouse in Brattleboro. This would have meant jobs for local residents. After three years of debate in which the company tried to come to terms with Act 250, they gave up and moved their warehouse forty miles down the road to Hatfield, Massachusetts. The small-town sanctity of Brattleboro was preserved but at the cost of about two hundred jobs.

In 1993, the citizens of St. Albans were faced with a tough

decision when Wal-Mart, an enormous discount department store, decided to set up shop in their town. Many Vermonters objected, certain that such a large store would ruin the character of their small towns and perhaps even put some old-time merchants out of business. As one longtime Burlington resident put it: "Everyone knows everyone in our downtown. I've gone to the same small shops for years. A place like Wal-Mart would put half of those guys out of business but fast." Or as Steve Keirnan of Burlington said: "The whole principle of this place is community."

The heads of Wal-Mart disagreed, claiming that "the evolution of the department store away from downtowns is as natural as the evolution of the horse and buggy to the automobile. Downtowns are functionally obsolete in their ability to serve the needs of today's consumer."

Most Vermonters feel their old-fashioned downtown shopping areas serve them just fine. In 1995, a young lawyer named William E. Roper took on Wal-Mart and after a lengthy legal battle forced the store to give up its designs on St. Albans. Once again, Vermon-

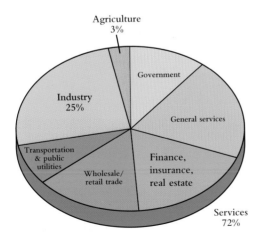

1992 GROSS STATE PRODUCT: $12 BILLION

ters were forced to choose what they valued more: money and jobs or the preservation of their state's small-town heritage and natural beauty.

When push comes to shove, Vermonters seem to opt for keeping the Wal-Marts of the world out. In the summer of 1995, the people of Chittenden went to the ballot box and voted by a ratio of 2 to 1 to sell four thousand acres of land to the Vermont national parks instead of to real-estate developers. Though this action deprived them of years of increased property tax revenue, it also kept their forest the way they liked it: undeveloped and beautiful. "People realized they had a natural playground," D. K. Smith notes, "and it was worth paying some extra taxes to keep it."

Economy vs. Environment. Economic concerns brush up against environmental ones on a nearly daily basis in Vermont. Killington Mountain recently wanted to expand its ski slopes, but Vermont logging companies wouldn't let them cut down the trees. In fact, Vermont ski slopes run into problems with fishermen every season when it comes time to make man-made snow. Snow-making uses a great deal of water, which depletes fish stock in the rivers.

As Vermont faces the twenty-first century, perhaps its greatest challenge is to reconcile its economic needs with its environmental concerns. And Vermonters know that they cannot afford in a very literal sense to let the rural character of their state fall by the wayside. As years have passed, Vermont has relied more and more on tourist dollars. Starting in the 1800s when tourists and famous writers such as Henry Wadsworth Longfellow took trains to Vermont's "mineral springs," the people of Vermont knew that they

Two skiers enjoy the slopes at Bolton Valley. Vermont makes nearly $1.5 billion a year from tourism.

could take economic advantage of their state's great natural beauty. The leaf peepers who visit each autumn and the skiers who descend upon their mountains each winter bring needed cash to Vermont.

The principal allure of the Green Mountain State is its beauty. Most Vermonters seem to realize that their greatest resource is their land. Without that, the tourist dollar will go elsewhere, and the economy would suffer greatly.

4 THE NATIVE VERMONTER

Vermont is not the state to visit if you like to meet people of different ethnic backgrounds. There are very few African Americans, Hispanics, or Asians here. One most definitely does not journey to the Green Mountain State for the Indian food or the sushi. Downtown Burlington does not sport a thriving Chinatown, and Middlebury has no Little Italy.

Vermont is not a place of great religious diversity either. Most Vermonters are Protestant. A staple of virtually every Vermont town is a church at the end of Main Street. There are pockets of Jews and Catholics, but they are in small number.

A LEGACY OF HARDSHIP

Despite the lack of diversity in the population, the Green Mountain State is the home of a distinctive group, commonly known as the native Vermonter.

And who might this be? Almost always a European Protestant whose family has spent generations in the state. But that's the simple answer—the tip of the iceberg. The Vermont native is a character who is the composite of many old-fashioned American values with a few New England quirks thrown in.

To understand the native Vermonter it is important to understand his or her roots. The life of the early Vermont settler was very

A woman taps a maple tree in Sheldon.

"Of this sap vast quantities of sugar are made, of a most delicious flavour, but great care is necessary in boiling down the sap, not to let it burn."
—John A. Graham, 1797

difficult. After all, the land was rocky, cold, and largely unpopulated. Settlers brave enough to move to Vermont were truly on their own. Often the father would come up alone in the summer, clear land, build a simple shelter, then move the family up in the winter. This is how one native settler named Batholomew Durkee described the process in 1770:

Goods and children were packed on hand sleds, which were hauled by the two parents, each wearing snowshoes. . . . This pioneer couple threaded the woods northward ten miles with their loads. They reached their log hut on March 6th, 1770. It was only partially roofed and had neither door nor window. Digging out the snow from the corner beneath the roofed part made a space for their beds.

But getting through winter was only the first step. Come spring, the rocky land had to be cleared, crops planted, and enough harvested to get the family through the following winter. It wasn't easy. Perhaps that's why one early settler, a Mrs. Gale, is quoted as saying that her life in Vermont wasn't part hardship but "all hardship."

It goes without saying that life in modern Vermont is not as difficult as it was two or three hundred years ago. Roads are mostly paved; homes are mostly heated. Even so, native Vermonters take life in the same spirit as their pioneer predecessors. Like his pioneer great-grandfather, the modern native knows that life is to be worked at rather than simply enjoyed. This sentiment is captured in a song called simply "Vermont" by Al Davis, of the local bluegrass group Banjo Dan in the Midnite Plowboys:

> Vermont I gave it all to you.
> Don't know what more that I could do.
> Broke my back and toiled upon your rocky soil.
> Now my heart and soul is going too.

HARD WORKERS

A native Vermonter knows that life is difficult. As one of Vermont's most fondly remembered governors, George Aiken, put it: "Problems are like a large rock in a farmer's field. He may hire a derrick to have it removed only to find two larger ones underneath. . . . But,

ETHNIC VERMONT

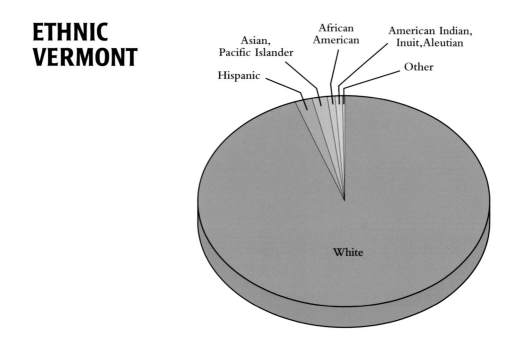

Asian,
Pacific Islander

African
American

American Indian,
Inuit, Aleutian

Hispanic

Other

White

after all, problems are what make life worth living." Aiken's sentiments serve as a kind of credo to the spirit of the native Vermonter. Under any rock lie two more rocks, probably larger than the first. The hard work that goes with tackling a difficult problem is what makes it fun to get up in the morning. Indeed, Vermonters don't avoid work. It is work that defines life.

Industry has been a motif that has run through Vermont life for years. The son of an old Vermonter named Darius Smith remembered that his father would rouse him each day with this cry: "Today is Monday, tomorrow is Tuesday, the next day is Wednesday, the week is half over and not a lick of work done yet." In 1880, Marshall Hapgood of Peru, Vermont, left these orders to his workers: "Put your whole mind, during business hours, upon business and business—only business alone. Tell no stories, listen to no

VERMONT HUMOR

What is Vermont humor? According to D. K. Smith, a native Vermonter and expert on the subject: "Vermont humor is a need for spice in what is a very simple, plain workaday life."

The traditional Vermont lifestyle was difficult, and the natives had to find humor in the chores they performed day after day, year after year. As Smith puts it: "Vermont humor stems from simple, unique insights into situations that might seem quite ordinary."

Here's an example: A chubby woman was married to an extremely thin farmer. One morning a neighbor saw her shaking a sheet out of a second-story window. "Hey, Mabel!" the man hollered. "If you're looking for your husband, he's out at the barn."

Vermonters can be very wry. Once a flatlander (meaning someone from out of state, usually a big city) moved to Vermont. Every morning he noticed a farmer with a team of horses that was pulling a single chain. After several months, the flatlander couldn't hold back his curiosity. What in the world were those horses doing with the chain? "Say, there!" he called one morning. "Why are your horses pulling that chain?" The Vermonter grinned. "Well," he replied. "I aint been able to teach 'em to push it."

Or the most famous of all Vermont jokes: An out-of-stater comes to a fork in the road. "Hey, there!" the out-of-stater yells to a farmer." Does it matter which road I take to Montpelier?" The Vermonter replies: "Not to me it don't."

The native Vermonter even has a sense of humor about his own heritage. "Have I lived in Vermont all my life?" a native might reply to a visitor. "Not yet, I haven't."

stories. . . . Consider every moment worth something and you will hit the mark."

Every moment is valuable to the Vermont native. As Governor

"I don't wait for moods. You accomplish nothing if you do that. Your mind must know it has got to get down to work." —Pearl Buck, Danby, 1950

Aiken said: "People ask what's the best time of year for pruning apple trees. I say 'when the saw is sharp.'" In other words, procrastination has no place in the Vermont mind-set. Assuming that every native Vermonter owns a sharp saw, the best time to get to work pruning an apple tree is right about now.

QUIET BUT NEIGHBORLY

Vermonters are generally men and women of few words. Given that the state's heritage is so intertwined with fighting the rocky soil and the harsh elements, Vermonters have developed a thick skin. An out-of-stater would be foolish to expect a Vermonter to suddenly gush out the details of her bad marriage or the trouble she's having controlling her teenage son. Therapists may be employed in the state but are generally not hired by the natives. If Vermonters want advice, they'll ask. Until then it is best to keep one's mouth shut. Indeed, a Vermonter will rarely meet a problem with a lot of discussion but, rather, with a wry grin and perhaps a shrug. If there is a blizzard and the temperature is below zero, the Vermonter will most likely put on his boots and grab a shovel. Talking isn't going to make the snow melt, but hard work will clear a path so the mailman can get to the door.

A real Vermonter will always speak his or her mind in the fewest words possible. Calvin Coolidge was a native Vermonter to the core. A story goes that while he was still president his Vermont neighbors wanted to celebrate his devotion to his hometown. Coolidge made the trip from Washington, D.C., and was presented with a handmade rake. "Hickory," the orator intoned, "like the President, is sturdy, strong, resilient, unbroken." Rather than accept the compliment with a polite nod, Coolidge looked the rake over, noticed that it wasn't made out of hickory but of ash, and scowled at the audience: "ASH!"

Though native Vermonters choose their words carefully, their quiet natures should not be confused with unfriendliness. Perhaps because Vermont is so small, Vermonters tend to be very neighborly. Native Vermonters will gladly donate a cord of wood in the winter. They will certainly call AAA and help fix a neighbor's car. They will invite in neighbors who have lost their power to use the

A horse-drawn sleigh was once the main form of winter transportation in Vermont. Some old-timers may still prefer it to a car. After all, a horse will always start and never gets ice on its windshield.

shower and do their wash. And Vermont volunteer fire departments have been heralded for their heroism and helpfulness beyond the call of duty.

PASTIMES

What do native Vermonters do in their spare time? There are many local customs, enjoyed by natives and visitors.

Contradancing, much like line dancing, is very popular in Vermont. It is not unusual to have a contradance on Saturday nights in the local Masonic Hall or church. A caller accompanied by a small band—usually a piano, guitar, and fiddle—teaches the steps then calls the dance. In keeping with Vermont community spirit, dancers switch partners often and then will usually all go out for dessert afterwards. Contradancing has been part of the Vermont experience for years and is still going strong.

Vermont is the home of the church supper. For a small fee, a church may sponsor a dinner to raise money. Common on Sunday

Church suppers in Peacham are usually potluck and always good.

MAPLE SUGARING

Vermont has long been America's home of maple sugar. Here are two recipes that use maple sugar. The first is from the church cookbook from the Trinity Mission of Trinity Church in Rutland. The year it was published? 1939!

Baked Beans with Maple Sugar
(a time-honored Vermont specialty)

Ingredients:
- 2 cups yellow-eyed beans
- 1/4 pound of heavy bacon
- 2 teaspoons salt
- 8 to 10 tablespoons of maple sugar
- 1 medium sliced onion
- 4 cups boiling water

Directions: Soak beans overnight, drain, then boil with 1/2 teaspoon baking soda to each quart of water; simmer slowly until skins burst; drain, add bacon and other ingredients, cover bean pot, and bake over low flame for 5 hours or more.* Eat.

Maple Squares

Ingredients:
- 3 beaten eggs
- 2/3 cup cooking oil
- 1 teaspoon vanilla
- 1 teaspoon baking powder
- 2 cups flour
- 1 cup maple syrup
- 1/2 teaspoon salt
- 1 cup of chocolate chips
- 1/2 cup of chopped walnuts

Directions: (this one is easy) Mix all the ingredients together and pour into greased 13 x 9 inch pan; bake at 350° for about 30 minutes.* Take out of the oven and eat.

*Ask an adult to help you when using the oven or stove.

nights, it is a chance for Vermonters to gather and chat. Another opportunity for Vermonters to socialize is in the fall during apple-picking season. Vermont is covered with apple orchards and exports a large part of its crop each year.

The native Vermonter also loves to hunt and fish. The NRA is a strong lobby in the Green Mountain State, and many natives own guns (though, unlike in many cities almost never use them against each other). Native Vermonters view hunting as one of their great rights, and the state is still full of enough deer and trout to keep most happy.

Another very popular sport in the state, especially among teenagers, is snowmobiling. The natives do ski, but many leave that more expensive sport to the out-of-staters. Gunning up the engine

Snowmobiling, Vermont's newest winter sport

of a snowmobile and racing it across a white pasture seems to be a more daring (if slightly dangerous and loud) form of entertainment. But not all native Vermonters are pleased that snowmobiling has found its way to their state — not by any means.

> If you want to meet a seventh-generation Vermonter, you'll see him astride his snowmobile, steering through somebody's field . . . as thoughtless as a teenager with a new driver's license and unrestricted use of the family car for an evening. He'll come through your land at night if he has a mind to, circling your house and making that infernal noise even if your house is dark and normal people might assume at that late hour that you're trying to sleep.
>
> —a seventh-generation Vermonter

ARTISTS

In the 1960s many members of the so-called flower-child generation decided they were fed up with city life and values and wanted the change of pace Vermont could provide. This influx of new blood brought many artists to the state to complement an already rich tradition. Some people believe that Vermont has more artists per capita than any other state in the nation.

Vermont has become the home of many writers. Aleksandr Solzhenitsyn, the well-known Russian author, settled there when thrown out of his homeland. J. D. Salinger, author of *The Catcher in the Rye*, has lived in seclusion in Vermont for years. More important may be the unknown writers who have flocked to the state. Vermont is the home of many young poets and would-be novelists as well as several noted writers' conferences.

Many musicians have made Vermont their home as well. Local

Aleksandr Solzhenitsyn, the famous Russian author of The Gulag Archipelago *and* The First Circle, *came to Vermont to live after he defected.*

music runs the gamut from bluegrass to folk to rock and is performed everywhere (in the summer, that is) at band shells, fairs, and picnics. Vermont has several small record labels dedicated to recording Vermont artists. Though not many Vermont bands have become popular out of the state, there is one exception. The rock band Phish got their start in a bar in Burlington.

Vermont is also known for its fine arts and crafts—beautiful homemade cups, bowls, and rugs. Frog Hollow in Middlebury has a year-round display of much of Vermont's finest wares. One of Vermont's best-known local artists, Woody Jackson, has achieved national prominence with his colorful and always creative rendering of one of Vermont's most enduring symbols: the cow. Jackson's cows can be seen around the country, especially on the cartons of Ben & Jerry's ice cream. Middlebury is the home of a store devoted entirely to his work.

NATIVES VS. NEW YORKERS

Frank Bryan and Bill Mares are two men who understand the psychology of the native Vermonter very well. As they write in their

The hard work continues even after the buckets have been hauled to the sugarhouse. Here two women fill cans with boiled down maple syrup.

book *Real Vermonters Don't Milk Goats*, real Vermonters don't comprehend "vacations, snow days, the 'fast lane,' second homes, psychotherapy, earrings on men, or brunch." Then again, Bryan and Mares note, real Vermonters are all born with "an inclination to say 'no,' patience, an ability to drive in the snow, no fear of the truth, a dexterity for milking cows blindfolded, and the proper pronunciation of the word 'ayup.' "

Bryan and Mares might also have noted that native Vermonters are born with a wariness of New Yorkers and those from other big cities. As John Garrison put it as early as 1946, "Vermont is a land filled with milk and maple syrup, and overrun with New Yorkers."

The influx of rich "city folk" remains one of the major tension points in the state today. Though the native Vermonter knows that these newcomers help the state's economy, how can he help but resent the rich city slicker gunning past his beat-up pickup truck in a bright red sports car?

The problems go deeper than petty jealousies or differences in lifestyle, though. Vermonters know that one of their main assets is the beauty of their state. It is that splendor that attracts these rich new Vermonters. But the Native Vermonter often isn't as concerned with her state's beauty as are her new neighbors. She's probably more worried about making ends meet.

Even so, compared to virtually every other state in the nation, Vermont's racial tensions are extremely minor. There have been no race riots in Vermont and virtually no serious racially motivated crimes. As the Green Mountain State enters the twenty-first century, it will have to work hard to keep its record this good. In the coming years it is quite likely that the state will be much more

Winter on Lake Champlain

ethnically diverse. It will be up to Vermont's people—natives, ex-New Yorkers, and newcomers of different races—to adapt and get going.

5 NOTABLE VERMONTERS

The Bread and Puppet Theater plays in Glover.

Famous Vermonters do not roll off the tongue as easily as well-known people from many other parts of America. Even so, the Green Mountain State has been the home of some well-known and interesting people.

THE SILENT PRESIDENT

Calvin Coolidge was president of the United States during the "Roaring Twenties," a time of great social upheaval and economic growth in the United States.

To most of the country, Coolidge was the epitome of the typical Vermonter: hardworking, frugal, and quiet. Born in Plymouth in 1872, "Silent Cal," as he came to be known, was an industrious young man who, according to his father, could get more sap out of a maple tree than anyone else in town. But Coolidge's overly serious demeanor caused some to comment that he had been "weaned on a pickle."

Coolidge turned to politics at a young age. Like most Vermonters of the era he was a Republican. After World War I, the country was tired of Woodrow Wilson's progressivism, and Warren G. Harding, a man who promised "a return to normalcy" was elected president. Harding turned to Coolidge, then the governor of Massachusetts, to be his vice president. Coolidge became president himself when Harding died of pneumonia.

Calvin Coolidge said that he saw his father show emotion only twice in his life: first, when Calvin's mother died; second, in 1923 when his father told him that Warren G. Harding had died in office and that he, Calvin, was now president of the United States.

A solid and honest citizen but not an inspiring leader, Coolidge took a "laissez-faire" approach to government, which allowed big business to do its will with little interference from the government. Theodore Roosevelt and Woodrow Wilson had expended great effort passing laws that tried to force the new, growing industries to spread the wealth and to create more humane conditions for their workers. Coolidge believed that "the business of America was business." To Coolidge's credit, however, his five years in office were times of great prosperity. The stock market boomed, and it seemed that everyone was getting rich.

In the end, Coolidge may have realized that the trappings of the presidency didn't suit a simple child of Vermont. In 1928, he decided against another four years in the White House, telling his supporters: "I do not choose to run for president in 1928." Those words may have been the wisest ones Coolidge ever spoke.

Like many politicians of his day, Coolidge often campaigned from the back of a train.

Herbert Hoover, the man who succeeded him, was soon slammed down by the stock market crash of 1929.

Despite his mixed reviews as president, no one ever doubted Coolidge's honesty and his commitment to the office. For these qualities, he remained a very popular figure in the state of Vermont until his death in 1933.

ROBERT FROST—AMERICA'S POET

Robert Frost was a poet whose life and verse came to exemplify the classic New England spirit. By the end of his long life, he had won the Pulitzer Prize for poetry four times. He read at President John F. Kennedy's inauguration and became America's unofficial poet laureate.

Despite his enormous success, Robert Frost was by no means an overnight success. Though he came to be closely identified with Vermont, where he made his home for the last several decades of his life, he was born in San Francisco. When Frost was just eleven, his father died, and the family moved to Lawrence, Massachusetts. Later, Frost spent short stints at Dartmouth and Harvard before settling with his wife in Derry, New Hampshire, where he became a chicken farmer.

But Frost was not put on earth to tend chickens. A horrible farmer, he got a job teaching English at Pinkerton Academy in Derry. These were crucial years for Frost. He read Emerson, took long walks in the woods, and wrote poems at night. As he said later in life, it was a time when he became "versed in country things."

After years of writing, a British publisher accepted his first two volumes of verse: *A Boy's Will* (1913) and *North of Boston* (1914). Still, Frost found it very difficult to make money. Though he spent most of his academic career teaching at numerous colleges, most frequently at Amherst, he considered his real home to be Vermont. After the death of his wife in 1938, Frost moved first to Shaftsbury (where he had bought a home in 1920), then to Ripton, where he helped found the successful Bread Loaf Writers' Conference. It was through Bread Loaf that Frost helped turn Vermont into a haven for some of America's best writers.

Many of Frost's best-known works have a New England setting. His poems deal with loss and the beauty of the land. "The Road

TWO POEMS BY ROBERT FROST

Spring Pools

These pools that, though in forests, still reflect
The total sky almost without defect,
And like the flowers beside them, chill and shiver,
Will like the flowers beside them soon be gone,
And yet not out by any brook or river,
But up by roots to bring dark foliage on.

The trees that have it in their pent-up buds
To darken nature and be summer woods—
Let them think twice before they use their powers
To blot out and drink up and seep away
These flowery waters and these watery flowers
From snow that melted only yesterday.

The Pasture

I'm going out to clean the pasture spring;
I'll only stop to rake the leaves away
(And wait to watch the water clear, I may):
I sha'n't be gone long.—You come too.

I'm going out to fetch the little calf
That's standing by the mother. It's so young
It totters when she licks it with her tongue.
I sha'n't be gone long.—You come too.

America's most celebrated poet, Robert Frost, in 1962

THE BREAD LOAF WRITERS' CONFERENCE

When Robert Frost was a young man he dreamed of owning a farm where he could write in the winters and entertain other writers "in a sort of summer literary camp" in the summers.

Frost's dream came true in August 1926 when the Bread Loaf Writers' Conference was founded by John Farrar, a thirty-year-old book and poetry editor. Set in the heart of the Green Mountains, Bread Loaf soon became one of the most important places for well-known and aspiring writers to meet, mingle, and share ideas. For two weeks a year during August, men and women of letters leave the city to come to Vermont for lectures, readings, workshops, and parties. The list of famous American writers who have found themselves at Bread Loaf at some point in their career is long, stretching from Willa Cather in the 1920s to Truman Capote in the 1940s to John Irving in the 1990s.

Through the years, the conference has maintained its commitment to cultivating literary excellence, doing its part to develop future generations of American writers.

Not Taken," one of Frost's most well-known poems, tells of a man who has to choose between two roads in "a yellow wood," one well traveled and one overgrown. Like most Vermonters, Frost elected to take "the road less traveled" which "made all the difference." In another of his famous poems, "The Gift Outright," Frost makes clear the strong connection he feels with the land: "The land was ours before we were the land's," a sentiment most Vermonters would share.

As Frost grew older, he became the grand old man of American poetry. His reputation was enormous, and young poets traveled to Bread Loaf Mountain for the chance to meet the great master. Only the brave would show him their work, though, for Frost could be a very tough critic.

Unfortunately, Frost's career success was undercut by personal tragedies: several children were stillborn or died very young. One of his two sons committed suicide. But like a true Vermonter, Frost persevered and poured his grief about his children's deaths into some of his best works, notably "Home Burial." And Frost found great solace in friendships. As he wrote in 1939: "Friends are everything. For why have we wings if not to seek friends at an elevation?"

Frost lived a long life, filled with great highs and lows, and died in January 1963.

EMPERORS OF ICE CREAM

Burlington is the birthplace of one of Vermont's sweetest new industries: Ben & Jerry's ice cream.

Ben Cohen and Jerry Greenfield met in the late 1960s while run-

The Emperors of Ice Cream, Ben and Jerry—perhaps the only businessmen ever to employ a "Joygang," workers hired to keep up company morale. Members of the Joygang have been known to give on-the-job back rubs!

ning laps in junior high in Merrick, Long Island. The two boys soon discovered a mutual hatred of gym class and a passion for ice cream. After college, they decided to do something daring and unusual. Proudly clutching diplomas from a five-dollar correspondence course in ice cream making from Pennsylvania State University, the two friends hoarded their life savings (all of eight thousand dollars), moved to Vermont, and turned a beat-up gas station into their first factory. Using Vermont's finest milk, cream, and sugar, it didn't take long for their ice cream to catch on. By the early 1980s, Ben & Jerry's was famous throughout Vermont. By the late 1980s, it was famous throughout the entire country. Now there are Ben & Jerry's scoop shops as far away as Israel and Russia.

Their enormous success is not due to luck. Ben and Jerry have used their imaginations to create an array of creative, offbeat flavors. There's the humorous Cherry Garcia, named for Jerry Garcia, the founder of the rock band Grateful Dead, along with Mint Oreo, Rainforest Crunch, Coffee Heath Bar Crunch . . . the list goes on and on.

More than just the wonderful flavors, however, makes Ben & Jerry's unique. As the two friends became more and more successful, they made a commitment to share their good fortune with their employees and community. In a program that Ben called "Caring Capitalism," seven and a half percent of the company's pretax profits are donated to a variety of worthy causes. On top of that, the company donates uncounted vats of ice cream each year. No one in the company is allowed to earn more than $75,000 a year—not even Ben and Jerry themselves (a very unusual policy in the age when most company president's pay themselves millions). Until recently, the company's highest paid executive could not earn more than seven times its lowest paid employee. Obviously, this is not a company that is devoted solely to profits. It is a business with a social conscience and a mission to replenish its community.

Ben and Jerry are representative of the kind of people who moved to Vermont in the 1960s. They are politically liberal and interested in social policy, not to mention perhaps the only businessmen to feature rock bands and free ice cream at their annual stockholder meetings. As Ben has been known to say, "If it's not fun, why do it?"

Undoubtedly, Ben & Jerry's is one of the great Vermont business success stories. People around the country still associate Vermont with maple sugar and cows, but in another few years, perhaps ice cream will be added to that list.

BERNIE SANDERS—POLITICAL MAVERICK

Leave it to Vermont to send the only member of the socialist party to the House of Representatives. Though born in Brooklyn, Bernie Sanders has been circulating in and out of Vermont politics for years. Unabashedly liberal in what is a historically conservative state, Sanders became mayor of Burlington in 1981, defeating old-time politician Gordon Paquette by ten votes.

Around the time he won election, Vermont underwent a huge real-estate boom. That meant more taxes and more money for the government to spend. Sanders put the extra cash to work in various creative ways geared toward helping the town's poorer residents. He put together a community medical center that supplies excellent health care for Burlington's poorer citizens and includes translators (including Vietnamese on Tuesday nights) for non-English speakers. Sanders also formed the Progressive Coalition—a liberal-minded political party that maintains a majority of city council seats in Burlington to this day. In fact, the head of economic development of the coalition, Peter Clavelle, is Burlington's current mayor.

Political maverick Bernie Sanders. Not a man who cares what others think, Sanders drove a beat-up car when he was mayor of Burlington. In fact, the car looked so old that a policeman gave it a ticket, assuming that someone was illegally using the mayor's personal parking space.

Not everything Sanders tried was a success. For instance he attempted to tax the university and hospital, both state institutions, to raise more money for his projects. And some Vermonters found his liberal policies too extreme. Even so, Sanders's eight year tenure as mayor was considered a definite success.

A few years later, Sanders set his sights on the United States House of Representatives and won election easily in 1992. Though still a socialist, Sanders votes with the Democrats on 95 percent of the issues. He is generally prounion, anticorporation. He is likely to favor anything that could possibly benefit the working man. And Sanders believes in his causes passionately. In fact, his voice is permanently damaged from years of shouting and arguing.

Vermonters seem to have a love/hate relationship with their sole representative. Though he always wins reelection by healthy margins, he is too liberal for many of the natives. His overly emotional appeals for the causes in which he believes can be embarrassing. On the other hand, Sanders is loved because he cares.

He typifies possibly more than anyone in the state the old-fashioned independent Vermont spirit: the willingness to fight for what he believes in and to work hard for what he sees as right for Vermont and the country.

6 SEASON BY SEASON

Children in Warren enjoy one of Vermont's many covered bridges.

You might say that Vermont is one of the most boring states in the country: It is always lovely. Virtually every Vermonter has a favorite quiet spot, usually off the beaten track — a small pond surrounded by maple trees or a pasture with an old stone fence where a horse and foal graze in the lazy summer sun.

Vermont is best experienced by the seasons. Each time of the year brings different and exciting things to do.

WINTER

Vermont's winters are not for the faint of heart. Still, if you can bundle up enough, there are many ways to enjoy the snowy outdoors.

Skiing. The first rope tow opened at a small mountain in Woodstock in 1934. Since that day, Vermont has become one of the most popular ski areas in the Northeast. In the south there is Mount Snow, in central Vermont, Killington and Pico. Farther north is Mansfield. Though Vermont's mountains are not tall by the standards of those who grew up out west, they make up in charm what they lack in sheer size. The trees are covered with sparkling white and dripping with icicles, and the views from the mountain tops are gorgeous. After an invigorating day on the slopes, it can be a great joy to take off your heavy ski boots and thaw out by a fire.

Many Vermonters enjoy the serenity of cross-country skiing: beautiful scenery, good exercise, and no lift lines.

Though it is downhill skiing that attracts the heavy tourist trade, many natives prefer cross-country. Vermont's winding paths and pastures make it easy to strap on a pair of skis and simply take off into the deep woods. Cross-country is much harder work than downhill but can be more rewarding—the warm fire feels even better at the end of the day.

One of the best cross-country areas in Vermont is at Stowe, near the Trapp Family Lodge. As most people know from the musical *The Sound of Music*, Maria Von Trapp escaped from the Nazis in World War II. What some people may not know is that Maria Von Trapp eventually found her way to Vermont, where she established perhaps the most successful resort in the state. Stowe remains one of Vermont's largest tourist attractions and holds a special allure for skiers. The Trapp Lodge along with Edson Hill Manor, Top Notch, and the Stowe Mountain Resort offer a series of interconnected cross-country trails that stretch deep into the mountains.

Lake Champlain. Most Vermonters grow up knowing how to ice-skate. After all, the state is covered with small lakes and ponds that are frozen for a good six months of the year. There is no better skating in Vermont than on its largest lake, Champlain. Gusts of wind sweep away the snow, leaving miles of clear ice.

Ice-skaters aren't the only people who enjoy Lake Champlain during the winter. As soon as the water freezes, fishermen drive trucks and cars onto the lake itself, drill holes in the thick ice and wait patiently for a nibble from the icy depths. In fact, many of these fishermen are so dedicated to their sport that they haul out a generator for electricity, erect a makeshift shack, and live on the ice for a good part of the winter. There are often so many fisher-men on the lakes that the lines of trucks and temporary homes are given actual street names! These fishermen give new meaning to the words "lakefront property."

Of course there is more to do in Vermont over the winter than ski, skate, and fish. Other popular sports include snowmobiling and good old-fashioned sledding. Mount Philo, in Charlotte about

An ice fisherman waits for a bite outside his winter home on Lake Champlain.

twenty minutes from Burlington, is perhaps one of the all-time great sledding hills. The long drive that winds up the side of the mountain is closed off for the winter, giving children and parents the luxury of barreling down a steep hill with no annoying cars and trucks hogging the road.

SPRING

Spring is a muddy time in Vermont—a season when cars get stuck and winter's trash still hasn't been cleaned up. Even so, a Vermont spring is the time to enjoy some of the states most time-honored traditions.

Maple Sugaring. Above all, Vermont is known for its maple sugar—the sweet candy that is made from the sap of a maple tree. It all starts around March 1, when a hole is drilled into a maple tree. As the temperature rises and the tree starts to come back to life, its clear sugar sap comes out of the hole and is collected in a bucket. The process is usually over by mid-April, for the syrup only flows out of the trees when the nights are below freezing and the days are warm.

Like most things in Vermont, maple sugaring is very hard work.

A man watches over a vat of boiling sap in a maple sugar house.

PAUL BUNYAN AND THE MAPLE-SUGARING BUSINESS

Here is a tall tale about Paul Bunyan, the great lumberjack. Once upon a time, Bunyan moved to Vermont to get into the maple-sugaring business. Back then the trees were so tall it took two men to see all the way to the top. Paul and his men tapped nearly half the maples in Vermont in a week. Unfortunately, a few of the workers didn't pull their weight and spent much of the time back in camp playing cards. Paul didn't know quite what to do. But lucky for him, in stepped Loudmouth Johnson, a nasty old businessman. He offered Paul's men a proposition.

"Come work for me!" Johnson declared one night at the men's camp. "I'll pay you a full quarter more a month than that skinflint, Bunyan!"

Well, Paul knew that good workers wouldn't jump ship for a measly twenty-five cents. But those few bad apples . . . well, they scooted over to Johnson's camp in a hurry. And with those lazy workers gone, Paul's men finished another quarter of the state in two days.

Then came the icing on the cake. One day while he was pulling sap buckets, one of Paul's assistants, Ford Fordsen ran up with amazing news.

"Paul!" he cried. "Loudmouth Johnson just got arrested. It seems that he and his crew used cow-milking machines to tap the trees!"

"Cow-milking machines?" Paul exclaimed.

"And that's not all!" Ford Fordsen continued. "Johnson's men tapped pine trees instead of maple. All their syrup turned into turpentine!"

Paul Bunyan laughed. "You know what, Ford?" he said. "Now I know that the men who stuck with me are native Vermonters. They work hard for a fair price and they know their maple from their pine."

With those words, the great man picked up a giant sap bucket and got back to work.

As Frank Buck of Pittsford tells it: "Buckets have to be hauled through muddy, cold woods. Tractors and trucks get stuck in that mud and the roads aren't really roads at all—more like rocky paths." And once the syrup is finally at the maple-sugaring house it must be brought to a fierce boil. It takes about forty gallons of maple syrup to make one gallon of maple sugar!

Yet, like all things in Vermont, hard work eventually pays off with a certain sweetness: in this case wonderful sap that Vermonters sell for more than $10 million annually. Vermont is dotted with maple-sugar houses—any visitor who wants a taste of the true Vermont experience should hunt one down.

Montpelier. Another spring tradition in Vermont is politics. A short walk down Main Street of the capital city of Montpelier (the smallest capital city in the country with only 8,247 residents) brings a visitor to an ornate building with a golden dome: the home of the legislature. Since Vermont's state representatives all have other jobs, the legislature is only open from January until April. Many issues have to be discussed and voted upon. As the April deadline approaches, the discussions turn into heated debates and out-and-out arguments. Any student of small government would do well to visit Montpelier in spring to get a firsthand dose of American democracy at work.

A Strange Contest. Each year in the middle of winter, the people of Danville walk out onto the frozen surface of Joe's Pond and place a large cinder block in the middle. Why? Well, the people of Danville don't need a groundhog to tell them how long winter will be. These Vermonters mark the beginning of spring by the moment the cinder block falls through the ice. The time is

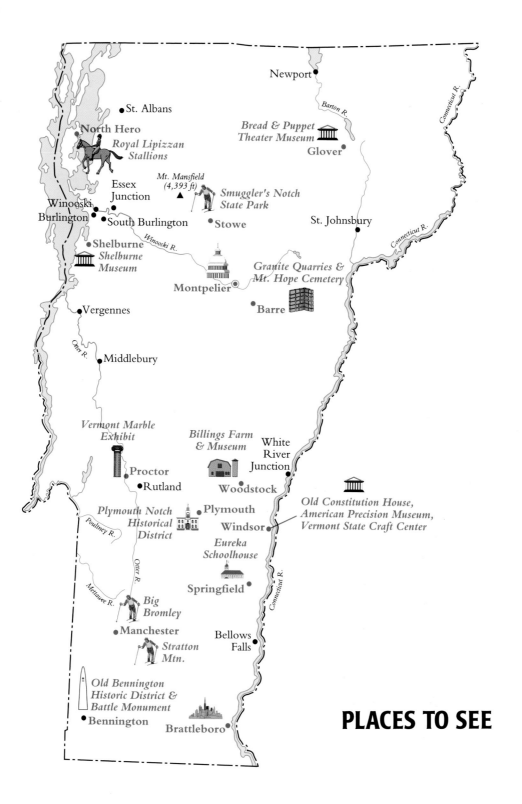

Newport

St. Albans

North Hero
Royal Lipizzan Stallions

Bread & Puppet Theater Museum
Glover

Barton R.

Connecticut R.

Essex Junction

Mt. Mansfield (4,393 ft)

Smuggler's Notch State Park

St. Johnsbury

Winooski
Burlington
South Burlington
Stowe

Connecticut R.

Shelburne
Shelburne Museum

Winooski R.

Montpelier

Granite Quarries & Mt. Hope Cemetery

Vergennes

Barre

Otter R.

Middlebury

Vermont Marble Exhibit

Billings Farm & Museum

White River Junction

Proctor
Rutland

Woodstock

Old Constitution House, American Precision Museum, Vermont State Craft Center

Plymouth Notch Historical District

Plymouth

Windsor

Poultney R.

Eureka Schoolhouse

Otter R.

Connecticut R.

Mettawee R.

Springfield

Big Bromley

Manchester

Bellows Falls

Stratton Mtn.

Old Bennington Historic District & Battle Monument

Bennington

Brattleboro

PLACES TO SEE

recorded to the second. An electrical wire is run from the block to a clock back on shore. The minute the block falls through, the cord is pulled and stops the clock.

Through the years, the cinder block at Joe's Pond has become something of a sensation. In 1996, three thousand people placed dollar bets (in a betting pool, winner take all) on when they thought the block would fall. As usual, the block fell during the last week of April. As that block crashed into the cold water, most Vermonters heaved a sigh of relief. Finally it was getting warm and just maybe winter was drawing to a close.

SUMMER

Summer in Vermont is filled with many wonderful things to do. Virtually anything that can be enjoyed outdoors is fair game.

Hiking. The Green Mountain State is a wonderful place to hike. The Long Trail wends its way from North Adams, Massachusetts, through Vermont and up into Canada. The mountains average between three and four thousand feet—high enough for spectacular views, but not too steep to climb. Perhaps the most distinctive mountain in the state is Camel's Hump, whose rock formation near the top is unmistakable from virtually any angle. The Crouching Lion is one of the only mountains in the state that is not part of a larger ski area. The hike up is not all that difficult, and the view from the top, which includes most of the Green Mountain range, is extraordinary.

The Northeast Kingdom holds another of Vermont's most stunning views: Lake Willoughby in Westmore. The lake is long and

Two children in Rochester get ready to go tubing.

narrow and surrounded by tall cliffs. A winding trail leads up the side of the cliffs to the top, where the view—like most in Vermont—is stunning.

The Water. Vermont is filled with hidden swimming holes and creeks. There is nothing quite so satisfying as coming across a brook with a deep swimming hole and taking a quick plunge. The water is usually a bit chilly, even in the summer, but nothing is more refreshing.

The Tunbridge Fair

Burr Pond in Pittsford is a good example of Vermont's many hidden treasures. Far from any major road, surrounded by deep woods, this small pond is completely secluded—too small for motorboats but plenty big to swim. There are hundreds like it in the state.

Swimming isn't the only way to enjoy Vermont's bodies of water. One of summer's great pleasures is drifting down a river in an inner tube. The White River at the junction of Route 107 and Route 100 in Stockbridge is one of the best places to give the sport of "tubing" a whirl. Floating northeast one passes pastures, woods, and bridges, from which you can dive into deep pools. The water is mostly calm with dashes of rapids thrown in to keep things interesting.

Festivals and Fairs. Summer in Vermont is a time of festivals and fairs. In late August and early September you can check out the Addison County Field Day and the Burlington's World Fair, two of the state's largest agricultural fairs, complete with prize-winning farm animals, racing pigs, tractor pulls, live music, and lots of good food.

Ben & Jerry's sponsors a fair that features folk and rock music at Sugarbush Mountain each summer. Burlington has a jazz festival each year in June. The Bread and Puppet Circus performs each July in Glover. This talented troupe uses giant puppets to put on shows that usually have some sort of political message.

Plymouth. One of the most serene places to visit during the summer is Calvin Coolidge's hometown of Plymouth. Preserved as it was in the 1920s when Coolidge was president, Plymouth retains its quaint Vermont charm. Down Main Street is a genuine, old-fashioned general store and a church, whose interior is all wood. Like everything else in the town, the church is devoid of any excess. Coolidge's homestead has been turned into a simple museum. The town is peaceful and pretty, and above all, modest— like Coolidge himself.

AUTUMN

Autumn is the season for which Vermont is famous. It is nearly impossible to even begin to pick a list of highlights. The entire state is beautiful from mid-September until late October.

Apple Orchards. But there is one thing that shouldn't be missed: apple orchards. With the trees in color many Vermonters enjoy taking a picnic out to a local apple orchard and picking apples. One of the biggest tourist attractions in the state (after Ben & Jerry's ice cream) is the Coldhollow Cider Mill in Waterbury. Run by a man who is a descendant of Vermont's first governor, Thomas Chittenden, this mill allows visitors to watch the apples being pressed and turned into cider.

Route 17. Grab a car (or get one of your parents to rent one) and take quiet Route 17 over the Appalachian Gap. With the trees turning, this is one of the prettiest drives in the state. The road twists and turns up the steep mountain, passing through an occasional small town. All of the Vermont staples are readily viewed—pastures, horses, farms. At the top of the gap the views of the valley below are tremendous. After drinking in the scenery, the drive down to Bristol on the other side is equally pretty. Once down the mountain, take a quick drive to the town of Middlebury

"To be a son of Vermont is glory enough for the greatest citizen."
—*Otto von Bismarck*

and walk across the Middlebury College campus. Middlebury is "the college on the hill" and affords excellent, quiet views of the foliage that surrounds it.

Bennington. Bennington is another of Vermont's college towns. Like all places in Vermont, Bennington is especially pretty in autumn. There are also several attractions of note. In the center

THE MORGAN HORSE

Along with maple sugar, the Morgan horse is one of the enduring symbols and prides of the state of Vermont.

"The Morgan Horse is one thing," the historian of the breed, Daniel Chipman Lindsey, asserted in 1857. "Every other horse is another."

The first of this great line of horses was born in 1789 in Springfield, Massachusetts and named after his master, Justin Morgan. Master and horse moved to Vermont in 1791. From this one animal sprang a breed of powerful descendants who could "outdraw, outrun, outwalk or outtrot" any other horses in the area. The hills of Vermont helped produce this rugged breed, giving the animals great muscle and endurance.

As time passed, the fame of the Morgan horse spread throughout the country. In 1909, the Morgan Horse Club was organized, where prizes were given for "conformity to the ancient Morgan type." One of the hardest tests was a 300-mile-long trail ride!

Over two hundred years later the Morgan Horse is still a source of great state pride. Their Vermont home is in Middlebury, though the sturdy breed has flourished at clubs all over the country.

of town is the monument to the Battle of Bennington. (The battle was actually fought five miles away near the town of Hoosick, New York.) Climb to the top of the obelisk, much like the Washington Monument (only smaller), for a lovely view of the surrounding area. Bennington is also the home of the Bennington Museum. Two galleries in the museum are devoted to Vermont-reared artist Grandma Moses. Those interested in seeing how children were educated in "the old days" can visit Moses' schoolhouse, which has been moved to the ground floor of the museum. The Bennington College campus is also worth a visit. The beauty of the leaves even makes the students feel better about going to class.

This list of Vermont attractions is by no means complete. Vermont is a wonderful state to explore. Go there and find your own favorite place.

THE FLAG: *Adopted in 1923, the flag shows the state coat of arms - a large pine tree, three sheaves of grain and a cow with mountains in the background.*

THE SEAL: *Adopted in 1779, the sea shows a pine tree with fourtee branches, representing the origina thirteen colonies and Vermont. Acros the center is a row of wooded hills. Th wavy lines at the top and bottom stan for sky and water and the sheaves o grain and the cow stand for agricultur*

STATE SURVEY

Statehood: March 4, 1791

Origin of Name: The name comes from the French words *Vert Mont*, which mean "Green Mountain."

Nickname: Green Mountain State

Capital: Montpelier

Motto: Freedom and Liberty

Bird: Hermit thrush

Animal: Morgan horse

Tree: Sugar maple

Flower: Red clover

Insect: Honey bee

Butterfly: Monarch butterfly

Hermit thrush

Red clover

GEOGRAPHY

Highest Point: 4,393 feet above sea level, at Mount Mansfield

Lowest Point: 95 feet above sea level, at Lake Champlain in Franklin County

HAIL, VERMONT!

Josephine Hovey Perry was one of more than a hundred people who, in 1937, submitted a song for consideration as the official state song. A committee had been appointed by Governor George D. Aiken in April of that year to make the selection. "Hail, Vermont!" was chosen and adopted on May 12, 1938.

By Josephine Hovey Perry

Area: 9, 615 square miles

Greatest Distance, North to South: 157.4 miles

Greatest Distance, East to West: 97 miles

Borders: New York to the west, Quebec, Canada, to the north, New Hampshire to the east, and Massachusetts to the south

Hottest Recorded Temperature: 105°F at Vernon on July 4, 1911

Coldest Recorded Temperature: -50°F at Bloomfield on December 30, 1933

Average Annual Precipitation: 39 inches

Major Rivers: Batten Kill, Connecticut, Lamoille, Missisquoi, Otter Creek, Winooski

Major Lakes: Bomoseen, Champlain, Memphremagog

Trees: ash, basswood, beech, birch, cedar, hemlock, maple, poplar, red pine, spruce, white pine

Wild Plants: anemone, arbutus, buttercup, daisy, gentian, goldenrod, lilac, pussy willow, red clover, violet

Animals: bear, beaver, bobcat, fox, mink, porcupine, rabbit, raccoon, skunk, squirrel, white-tailed deer, woodchuck

Birds: bluebird, cardinal, chickadee, finch, goose, gray or Canada jay, grosbeak, hummingbird, loon, martin, oriole, raven, robin, thrush

Fish: bream, carp, catfish, eel, perch, salmon, sheepshead, trout

Endangered Animals: bald eagle, common loon, common tern, eastern mountain lion, five-lined skink, Henslow's sparrow, Indiana bat, lake sturgeon, loggerhead shrike, lynx, marten, osprey, peregrine falcon, spruce grouse, striped chorus frog, timber rattlesnake

Skink

Endangered Plants: bearberry willow, Champlain beach grass, climbing fern, mare's-tail, moss, needle-spine rose, peatmoss, swamp birch, scrub oak

TIMELINE

Vermont History

c. 1300-1750 Iroquois and Algonquian-speaking tribes settle in region

1609 Samuel de Champlain claims for France the area that will become Vermont

Early 1600s Algonquians, with the help of the French, defeat their enemy, the Iroquois

1666 French dedicate fort to Saint Anne on Isle La Motte, Lake Champlain

1690 Fort established at Chimney Point, near Middlebury

1724 First permanent European settlement made at Fort Dummer, now Brattleboro

1749-1763 Royal governors of New Hampshire and New York claim the same parts of present-day Vermont and make grants of this land, starting the longstanding battle of the grants

1754-1763 French and Indian Wars fought between England and France with aid of Indian allies; British take control of Vermont

1764 England recognizes New York land grants

1770 Green Mountain Boys formed to fight New York settlers

1775 Revolutionary War begins in Massachusetts

1775 Ethan Allen and Green Mountain Boys capture Fort Ticonderoga from British

1777 Vermont settlers declare territory to be an independent republic

1790 New York land claims settled

1791 Vermont becomes fourteenth state

1805 Montpelier becomes capital

1812-1814 War of 1812 between the United States and Great Britain

1823 Champlain Canal between Lake Champlain and Hudson River allows Vermont farmers to ship goods to New York City

1830 Chester A. Arthur born in Fairfield

1861-1865 Civil War between the North and the South

1864 Confederate raid on St. Albans, northernmost land action of the war

1872 Calvin Coolidge born in Plymouth Notch

1881 Chester A. Arthur becomes twenty-first president after James Garfield is assassinated

1896 Vermont becomes first state to institute absentee voting

1911 Vermont becomes first state with publicity bureau to attract tourists

1914-1918 World War I

1923 Calvin Coolidge becomes thirtieth president of the United States when Warren G. Harding dies in office

1927 Worst flood in Vermont history causes 60 deaths and millions of dollars in damage

1939-1945 World War II

1960s Interstate highway between Massachusetts and Vermont contributes to growth of industry and tourism

1970 Legislature passes Environmental Control Law, allowing state to restrict major development that could harm environment

1974 Patrick J. Leahy becomes first Democrat elected to U.S. Senate since early 1880s

1984 Madeleine M. Kunin becomes first woman elected governor of Vermont

1991 State celebrates its bicentennial

ECONOMY

Agricultural Products: apples, corn, greenhouse products, hay, maple syrup, milk, oats, potatoes, poultry

Manufactured Products: computers and computer parts, electrical equipment, machine tools, machinery, paper products, printed materials, transportation equipment

Maple syrup

Natural Resources: granite, gravel, limestone, marble, sand, slate, talc, timber

Business and Trade: community, social, and personal services; finance, insurance, real estate; retail and wholesale trade; transportation, communications, and tourism

CALENDAR OF CELEBRATIONS

Okemo Winter Festival For nine days in January, Okemo celebrates winter with tobogganing, snow sculptures, ski races, torchlight parades, and fireworks.

Stowe Winter Carnival This winter carnival in mid-January is one of the oldest village winter celebrations in the United States, with snow sculptures, dog sled and ski races, and other events.

Maple Sugar Festival April means maple sugar time, especially in St. Albans, where a three-day festival includes sugarhouse demonstrations of the boiling process, arts and crafts, antiques, and other events.

Lake Champlain Balloon and Craft Festival Hot air balloons at the Champlain Valley Fairgrounds take off every May on Memorial Day weekend. The festival also includes skydivers, a crafts fair, and children's rides.

Summer Fest at Mount Snow Throughout July and August, ballet, children's shows, and concerts by folk, jazz, and classical artists are staged at the base lodge of the Mount Snow ski resort in Dover.

Old Rockingham Days This full August weekend of events in Rockingham features live entertainment, dancing, fireworks, and contests.

Domestic Resurrection Circus For a week in August, people gather in Glover at the Bread and Puppet Theater to take part in a festival about the struggle between good and evil. It ends with a parade of the giant puppets.

Tunbridge Little World's Fair This four-day celebration, dating back to 1867, brings thousands of visitors to the tiny village of Tunbridge each September. The fair has carnival rides and games, livestock displays, dancing, a fiddlers' contest, horse pulls, and other competitions.

State Fair In early September, Rutland is host to the annual state fair, with its carnival rides, exhibits, races, tractor pulls, and other events.

Lumberjack roundup, Rutland

National Championship Fiddle Contest Held in Barre in late September, this is the finale of a summer of fiddling contests throughout Vermont— the fiddling capital of the entire East coast.

Annual Wild Game Supper For decades, visitors have crowded into the town of Bradford on the Saturday before Thanksgiving for a meal of wild game— buffalo, venison, moose, pheasant, coon, rabbit, wild boar, and bear.

STATE STARS

Ethan Allen (1738-1789) and his Green Mountain Boys joined forces with Benedict Arnold's Connecticut troops to capture Fort Ticonderoga from the British in 1775. Allen was born in Litchfield, Connecticut, and later settled in the New Hampshire land-grant territory, now Vermont, where he organized the Green Mountain Boys to drive off New York settlers.

Chester A. Arthur (1830-1886) became the twenty-first president of the United States when he succeeded James A. Garfield, who was assassinated in office. Arthur, born in Fairfield, is best known for working to modernize the navy and for signing the Civil Service Act, which changed the way public offices were filled.

Chester A. Arthur

Frederick Billings (1823-1890), a lawyer and businessman born in Royalton, was president of the Northern Pacific Railway. He extended the railroad line from Bismarck in the Dakota Territory to the Columbia River. Billings, Montana, was named for this Vermont native.

Thomas Chittenden (1730-1797), born in East Guilford, Connecticut, was Vermont's first governor. He was a leading figure in the establishment of Vermont as an independent territory and later helped win its admittance into the Union. He served as governor of the republic from 1778 to 1789 and from 1790 to 1791, and then as governor of the new state of Vermont from 1791 to 1797.

Calvin Coolidge (1872-1933), born in Plymouth, became the thirtieth president of the United States in 1923, succeeding Warren G. Harding, who died in office. Elected to a full term in 1924, Coolidge was known for his honest, simple manner and his strong support of business; he once said, "The business of America is business." Coolidge refused to run again in 1928.

Thomas Davenport (1802-1851), an inventor, born in Williamstown, was a blacksmith by trade. Fascinated by the electromagnet, he invented a way to turn electromagnetic force into mechanical power. He is credited with developing the first electric motor in 1834 and the first model of an electric car.

John Deere

John Deere (1804-1886), blacksmith, inventor, and manufacturer, was born in Rutland. He moved to Illinois in 1837, where he invented the first successful steel plow from an old saw blade after hearing local farmers complain that the state's heavy soil stuck to their iron and wood plows. Deere's invention improved farming throughout the Midwest.

George Dewey

George Dewey (1837-1917), born in Montpelier, commanded the U.S. Asian squadron during the Spanish American War and in 1898 captured Manila in the Philippines. He was later promoted to the rank of admiral of the Navy, a rank created especially for him.

John Dewey (1859-1952), born in Burlington, was a philosopher, writer, psychologist, and educator. He is considered the founder of the education movement that stresses learning through experience and activity rather than through traditional drill, lecture, and memorization.

Stephen A. Douglas (1813-1861), at five foot four, was known as "the little giant." He was born in Brandon and moved to Illinois as a young man.

Stephen A. Douglas

His debates with Abraham Lincoln for the Senate seat from Illinois in 1858 brought Lincoln to national attention. Douglas served in the U.S. House of Representatives from 1843 to 1847 and in the Senate from 1847 to 1861. He also ran unsuccessfully for president against Lincoln in 1860.

Dorothy Canfield Fisher (1879-1958) was a popular writer whose fiction included *The Brimming Cup, The Homemaker,* and *Four Square.* She was also author of the nonfiction work *Vermont Tradition: The Biography of an Outlook on Life.* Fisher was born in Lawrence, Kansas, and moved to Arlington, Vermont, in 1907.

Robert Frost (1874-1963), a poet, was born in San Francisco, California, but lived in Vermont much of his adult life. He won four Pulitzer Prizes in poetry. Some of his most famous poems are "The Road Not Taken," "Mending Wall," and "Stopping by Woods on a Snowy Evening."

Paul Harris (1868-1947) was a lawyer and the founder of Rotary International. Born in Racine, Wisconsin, Harris grew up in Vermont. After moving to Chicago, he felt isolated and formed a club with a handful of other associates. The meeting rotated from office to office and was called the Rotary Club. The idea spread to other cities, and by 1910 the National Association of Rotary Clubs was formed, with Harris as president.

Richard Morris Hunt (1827-1895), an architect, was born in Brattleboro. He designed many landmark buildings in New York City, including Presbyterian Hospital, the Tribune Building, and Lenox Library. He also designed many mansions, including the Vanderbilt family's 225-room Biltmore House in Asheville, North Carolina. He is called the "dean of American architecture" because of his work in advancing the field's educational and professional standards.

Madeleine Kunin (1933-   ), born in Zurich, Switzerland, was the first woman governor of Vermont, serving from 1985 to 1991. As governor, she reduced the state debt, enforced a stricter environmental code, and actively recruited women to work in state government. In 1994, she published *Living a Political Life: A Memoir.*

Sinclair Lewis (1885-1951) won the Nobel Prize in literature in 1930 for his novels, which included *Elmer Gantry, Main Street, Dodsworth, Babbitt,* and *It Can't Happen Here.* The latter novel was set in Vermont. Lewis was born in Sauk Center, Minnesota, and was living in Barnard, Vermont, when he won the Pulitzer Prize in literature.

Sinclair Lewis with Dorothy Thompson

Levi Parsons Morton (1824-1920), born in Shoreham, served as vice president of the United States under President Benjamin Harrison from 1889-1893. He then served as governor of New York from 1895 to 1897.

Clarina Howard Nichols (1810-1885) was a newspaper woman who wrote editorials in support of the women's suffrage movement and lobbied to improve laws concerning women. She was born in West Townshend.

John Humphrey Noyes (1811-1886), a social reformer, was born in Brattleboro. He founded the utopian Oneida community in central New York. The community practiced "complex marriage" in which all men and women were considered to be married to one another.

Elisha Graves Otis (1811-1861), born in Halifax, Vermont, developed the first mechanical elevator with a safety device to prevent it from falling if the chain broke. After his company, Otis Elevator, installed the first safe passenger elevator in a New York City store, the elevator gained popularity and brought major changes in construction and architecture. The elevator helped make the skyscraper possible.

Joseph Smith (1805-1844) was the founder of the Church of Jesus Christ of Latter Day Saints, known as the Mormon Church. Born in Sharon, Smith moved to Palmyra, New York, in 1816. He claimed to see visions and said that one of these visions led him to a hill in Manchester, New York, where he discovered golden plates on which were inscribed the history of the true church of America as carried by ancient Indian descendants of the lost tribes of Israel. Smith deciphered and translated these plates into *The Book of Mormon*, published in 1830.

Joseph Smith

Aleksandr Solzhenitsyn (1918-　　), winner of the Nobel Prize in literature in 1970, was born in the former Soviet Union. He was exiled from the Soviet Union and moved to the United States to live on a farm near Cavendish. He wrote *Cancer Ward*, *The Gulag Archipelago*, and *The First Circle*.

Dorothy Thompson (1894-1961), newspaper columnist and writer, was born in Lancaster, New York, but lived in Barnard for many decades. She was one of America's most powerful voices against Hitler and the Nazis. She also wrote many books, including *New Russia*, *I Saw Hitler*, and *Let the Record Speak*.

Rudy Vallee (1901-1986), born in Island Pond, became one of the nation's most popular "crooners" (singers) in the 1920s. He was a star of radio and movies.

Rudy Vallee

Henry Wells (1805-1878), born in Thetford, merged competing companies into the American Express Company in 1850 and organized Wells, Fargo & Company two years later.

Brigham Young (1801-1877), born in Whitingham, became the leader of the Church of Jesus Christ of Latter Day Saints upon the death of Joseph Smith. He led the emigration of the Mormon Church to Utah in 1848. Young and the Mormon church became a strong economic force, and when Utah became a territory in 1850, Young was appointed its governor by President James Buchanan. He remained governor until 1857, when he was replaced because of political differences. However, his influence throughout Utah remained strong because of his leadership of the church.

Brigham Young

TOUR THE STATE

Mount Mansfield (Stowe area) The highest point in Vermont provides a spectacular view of the state. In the summer the peak can be reached by a toll road or by an eight-passenger gondola.

Ben & Jerry's Ice Cream Factory (Waterbury) Tour the plant where ice cream is produced, learn fun facts about cows, and sample the ice cream.

Smuggler's Notch (near Stowe) This pass between Mount Mansfield and the Sterling Mountains was named during the War of 1812, when smugglers carried goods between Canada and Boston, Massachusetts. This area is now open for hiking and exploration of rock formations such as the Smuggler's Cave, Smuggler's Face, and the Hunter and His Dog.

The Fairbanks Museum and Planetarium (St. Johnsbury) The museum features a hall with 3,000 preserved animals, as well as exhibits from the nineteenth century from all over the world. A planetarium and exhibits of Vermont history and nature are also popular.

Bread and Puppet Theater Museum (Glover) The world-famous Bread and Puppet Theatre troupe lives here in Glover, where its larger-than-life puppets of giants, dwarfs, and other creatures are displayed.

Maple Grove Maple Museum (St. Johnsbury) Watch maple candy being produced in the "world's largest maple candy factory," which has been in business since 1904.

Covered Bridges (Lyndonville) Vermont is well known for its covered bridges. Five are found in this village, including one 120-foot bridge built in 1865 and another built in 1869 and later moved to its present site.

Plymouth Notch Historical District (Plymouth) Calvin Coolidge, the thirtieth president of the United States, was born here in 1872. Visitors can see his homestead and explore the recreated general store that Coolidge's father once ran.

Granite Quarries and Mount Hope Cemetery (Barre) Visitors can watch as large blocks of granite are quarried, sawed, polished, and cut. At the Mount Hope Cemetery, elaborate memorials have been sculpted by local stonecutters in honor of their families.

Montshire Museum of Science (Norwich) This extensive science museum offers hands-on exhibits and an aquarium of New England fish, an ant colony, a kinetic energy machine, workshops, hikes, and special events.

Eureka Schoolhouse (Springfield) The schoolhouse is the oldest in the state and one of the few remaining Vermont public buildings from the eighteenth century.

Windsor-Cornish Covered Bridge. Built in 1866, this is the longest covered bridge in the state.

Billings Farm & Museum (Woodstock) You can view the operations of an 1890s' farm, including plowing, seeding, cultivating, harvesting, making cheese and butter, woodcutting, and sugaring. Visitors can also learn about how modern dairy farms are run.

Bennington Museum (Bennington) Historic items from the Battle of Bennington are exhibited, including the oldest American Revolutionary flag in existence, along with early American glass, furniture, dolls, toys, and pottery.

Bennington Battle Monument (Bennington) The 306-foot granite tower, one of the world's highest battle monuments, honors colonists who

Revolutionary War Memorial, Bennington

defeated the British in the Battle of Bennington in 1777.

Vermont Marble Exhibit (Proctor) One of the world's largest quarries and one of the biggest tourist attractions in New England, it offers a view of the various stages of transformation of the stone from rough cut blocks to polished slabs, as well as a large collection of marble.

Shelburne Museum (Shelburne) This reconstruction of early American life fills 35 buildings, including a general store, jail, and saw mill. A 1915 steam locomotive, the steamship *Ticonderoga*, paintings, carriages, rugs, textiles, and toys are also on display.

Old Red Mill (Jericho Corners) Built in the 1800s and set above a gorge, Old Red Mill is one of the most photographed buildings in the state. It houses a large photography exhibit, including the photographs of Wilson A. "Snowflake" Bentley, a farmer who was the first person in the world to photograph individual snowflakes.

Royal Lipizzan Stallions (North Hero) These dazzling white horses, first bred in the sixteenth century in Austria, are trained to perform intricate moves. Each summer, from mid-July through August, horses and riders put on a show in North Hero.

FIND OUT MORE

Want to know more about Vermont? Check the library or bookstore for these titles:

STATE BOOKS

Bearse, Ray. *Vermont: A Guide to the Green Mountain State*. Boston: Houghton Mifflin, 1966.

Bryan, Frank and Bill Mares. *Out of Order! The Very Unofficial Vermont State House Archives*. Shelburne: New England Press, 1991.

Bryan, Frank and Bill Mares. *Real Vermonters Don't Milk Goats*. Shelburne: New England Press, 1983.

Conner, Judson J. *Vermont from A to Z*. Shelburne: New England Press, 1990.

Davis, Dean C. *Justice in the Mountains*. Shelburne: New England Press, 1980.

Green Mountain Club. *Guide Book to the Long Trail*. Montpelier: Green Mountain Club, 1985.

Hill, Ralph N., Murray Hoyt, and Walter R. Hard, Jr. *Vermont, A Special World*. Montpelier: Vermont Life Magazine, 1983.

McNair, Sylvia. *America the Beautiful: Vermont.* Chicago: Childrens Press, 1991.

Morrissey, Charles T. *Vermont: A History.* New York: W. W. Norton, 1984.

Pelta, Kathy. *Vermont.* Minneapolis: Lerner Publications, 1994.

Perrin, Noel. *Vermont.* New York: Viking Press, 1973.

Shepard, Suzanne Church, ed. *The Vermont Almanac.* Middlebury: Regional Facts, Inc., 1993.

SPECIAL INTEREST BOOKS

Frost, Robert. *Birches.* Young, Ed., Illus. New York: Henry Holt, 1988.

————. *Stopping by Woods on a Snowy Evening.* Jeffers, Susan, Illus. New York: Dutton Children's Books, 1978.

Jellison, Charles A. *Ethan Allen: Frontier Rebel.* 1969 Reprint, Syracuse: Syracuse University Press, 1983.

Henry, Marguerite. *Justin Morgan Had a Horse.* 2nd ed. New York: Macmillan, 1991.

INDEX

Page numbers for illustrations are in boldface.